Mike Colman is a senior sportswriter for the *Courier-Mail* and *Sunday Mail* in Brisbane. He has written several books including the best-selling *Fatty – The Strife and Times of Paul Vautin*, *Super League – The Inside Story* and the award-winning *Eddie Gilbert – The True Story of an Aboriginal Cricketing Legend* with Ken Edwards.

RAGING BULL

RAGING BULL

GORDEN TALLIS

WITH MIKE COLMAN

MACMILLAN
Pan Macmillan Australia

First published 2003 in Macmillan by Pan Macmillan Australia Pty Limited
St Martins Tower, 31 Market Street, Sydney

National Library of Australia
Cataloguing-in-Publication data:

Colman, Mike.
Raging bull: the Gorden Tallis story.

ISBN 0 7329 1185 0.

1. Tallis, Gorden. 2. Rugby League football players – Australia – Biography.
3. Rugby football players – Australia – Biography. I. Colman, Mike. II. Title.

796.333092

Typeset in 12/16 pt Janson Text by Post Pre-press Group
Printed in Australia by McPherson's Printing Group

Contents

Acknowledgements

As with all projects of this kind, *Raging Bull* could not have been completed without the assistance of a large number of people. We would particularly like to thank the following for the part they played in making this book a reality:

Christine Tallis, Judy Tallis, Wayne Bennett, Rod Reddy, Brian Smith, Geoff Carr, Chris Anderson, Craig Bellamy, George Mimis and all of Gorden's family, team-mates and friends who contributed to the story which appears on the following pages.

We would also like to thank the team at Pan Macmillan, notably Tom Gilliatt and Clare Wallis, for their encouragement and expertise in producing a book we can all be proud of.

Gorden Tallis and Mike Colman
June, 2003

16 March 2003
Penrith Football
Stadium

Round 1, 2003, early in the second half, and I'm lying on my back with someone choking me. He abuses me, and when we get to our feet I grab his jumper. He tries to pull away and I say, 'You're a tough man when I'm on my back, aren't you.' He says something back and turns away so I wait until he's facing me and I smash him on the side of the head. Again and again. He gets one in too and we keep going at it until players from both sides get between us and grab our arms. The ref calls us out and points to the sheds. Even before we start walking the crowd is screaming at me. As I get close enough I can see their faces all twisted up with

1

hatred as they call me every name you can think of. They start throwing stuff. Cans and bottles. Luckily there is a wire cage between me and them, but some still try to spit on me. They are fired up, having the time of their lives, and so am I. I love it.

There's a thin red line in rugby league between what your coach expects and what the game's administrators and the critics think is acceptable. The trick is to walk that line without crossing over. Sometimes it's easier said than done.

When you get to the top, you want to stay there as long as you can, and that's why I fight so hard to keep my place in the game. I know I'm not a brilliant player, not like a Darren Lockyer or an Andrew Johns. I can't make something out of nothing, spear through a gap or put a bloke through a hole. That's not my job. My job is to physically intimidate the opposition.

That's how I got myself on to front pages and talkback radio all over the country after that first round match against Penrith. A young bloke whose name I didn't even know had tackled me and had his hand on my throat, pushing as hard as he could. I couldn't breathe, and as he got up he said something like, 'You're a mongrel and you can't play.' That's fair enough. I've heard a lot worse than that in over a decade of first grade rugby league, but having heard that, and other things that he had said in the game, it was up to me to react. And believe me, no matter what people were saying over the week that followed, I had to react. As I said earlier, that's my job.

I suppose I could let him get away with what he was doing. I could get to my feet, play the ball and get on with the game. I could work on my 'anger management', as someone in the media said, but that would send a message – not just to him, but to every other player in the competition – that I'd gone soft, that I wasn't someone to be respected any more. More than that, it would send a message to all the coaches in the competition that I wasn't prepared to stand up for myself or my team. It gets back to walking that thin line. Every physical player in the game tries to do it; some manage better than others. Adrian Morley from the Roosters does it better than just about anyone I have ever seen.

That's why I hit that kid. Like a lot of things I've done in my career, I'm sorry that it was on TV. I'm sorry that it became something for the media to get all excited about and I'm sorry if some mother thinks rugby league isn't a good game for her little boy to play because of it. But I don't regret it for a second. I can't afford to; it's my job.

You might have noticed that not one coach had anything bad to say about that fight. That's because they know that if they want to have a winning football team they need someone who the other players respect and fear. No, the people who were complaining were the ones who don't understand the game of rugby league. I heard one bloke on radio say that I shouldn't have to do that sort of thing. He said, 'Darren Lockyer doesn't do it.' Darren Lockyer doesn't do it because that's not what he is in the team to do. It is not his role, it's mine, and if I do my job properly, it will give Darren more room to do his. Darren is there to make breaks, reverse the play, set up attacks. The day he doesn't do that, just like the day a goal-kicker stops kicking goals, a tackling machine starts dropping off tackles – or a hard man just lies there and cops it – is the day the coach starts looking around for someone else.

If that bloke on radio wants to see the game played between two teams of Darren Lockyers, good luck to him. But it won't be rugby league. It won't be the game that I play.

As far as Ben Ross, that kid from Penrith, was concerned, he was showing me a lack of respect. He was shooting his mouth off and taking cheap shots. He wanted to show me, and everyone else, that he was tougher than me. But the thing is, you don't get respect in rugby league by what you say, you get it by what you do. That kid might get to the top one day – I noticed that the week after our fight he managed to get his picture on the front cover of *Rugby League Week* – but I'll tell you one thing, he won't get it at my expense and he won't get it easily. You have to earn it in our game.

There are plenty of hard men in rugby league, men I respect. Take Ruben Wiki. I think he is a tough man, and whenever I play him I show him respect. When we cross paths for the first time in a game, whether it is in a tackle or jogging to a scrum, I'll tap him on the arm and give him a nod, like, 'G'day mate, how ya going?' I wouldn't expect him to put a cheap shot on me and he knows I wouldn't put one on him. After that fight against the Penrith bloke someone wrote to a newspaper and said I was gutless for belting a kid. They said I wouldn't have the guts to take on someone like Solomon Haumono. I say I would, but the thing is, I wouldn't have to, because we are friends and we respect each other. There are other men like that. You'll find at least one in every top team, just like you'll find a good playmaker, a good goal-kicker, good 'up the middle' ground gainers and all the other elements that make up a team.

Don't think throwing punches has anything to do with being a hard man either. Some of the toughest men I have ever seen play rugby league have been the smallest. Blokes like Geoff Toovey, who was tiny but never took a backward step, or Alfie Langer, who would tackle anyone, no matter how much bigger than him they were. Others are tough because they play through pain. Someone like Kevin Campion, who doesn't think he has been in a game if he hasn't ended up with more stitches than my wife's wedding gown. Or Mick De Vere, who played nearly a full game with a broken cheek and made himself available for the next match as well.

Those are the type of players I respect; players who will do their jobs no matter what the odds against them are. I suppose that is the type of player I would like to be too. I know sometimes I go a bit too far in some people's opinion, but that is just the passion I put into the game. It is that passion which has seen me clash with referees and throw a few punches if I think someone is trying to stand over me or my team. It is also the passion which makes me say what I feel, because I care a lot about the game I play. If any of that gets me into trouble, I'll wear it.

I have to laugh when I get myself into strife and everyone has an opinion about what was going through my mind at the time or what sort of person I am. Those people don't know me. They don't know what made me who I am. To do that, they would have had to be there at the beginning . . .

CHAPTER ONE

WHERE'S WALLY?

When I was growing up in Townsville there were two gun footballers in my family. And I wasn't one of them.

My dad Wally was a bit of a local legend. Not that he'd tell you. Dad's not one to sit down and talk about his career, but there are plenty of other people who'll do it for him. Every time I'm up in North Queensland people come up to me and say: 'You'll never be as good as your old man', or 'Geez your dad could kick a ball.'

That ability to kick a ball probably came from his Aussie Rules background. Dad played 300 games of A grade Aussie Rules for the Garbutt Magpies on Saturdays, and league as a fullback for Souths, WEAs, Brothers and Centrals on Sundays until he retired, at 37. He made a comeback at 40 but my mum Judy grabbed him at half-time and said she'd burn his boots if he went back on, so he stayed off for the second half and that was the end of his playing days.

Mum and Dad met through football. She had three brothers who played for the Magpies, and when she was about nine or ten she went along to watch them and spotted Wally Tallis, who was five years older. By the time he was 16 or 17 he was playing A grade and Mum was his number one fan. Dad played for North Queensland for two seasons – 1962 and 1963 – and then went to England for two years with Leigh Rugby League Club in Lancashire before coming back to Townsville and playing out the rest of his career there. After that he became a junior coach, in charge of the Townsville Under 19 side for ten years. He coached Gene Miles, Colin Scott, Terry Butler, Chris and Pat Phelan, and Mark and Gavin Payne. Seven of his teams won the Foley Shield Under 19 championship, and in the 1980s he was president when the Centrals brought Rod Reddy back to Townsville as captain–coach.

Mum and Dad got married when Dad came back from England. They were married on a Saturday and Dad played Foley Shield the next day. When he wasn't playing footy, Dad worked in the spare parts department of a local air-conditioning company. When we kids got older, Mum went to work in the laundry at Park Haven Hospital – she stayed there for 21 years.

People ask me about my ethnic background. Newspapers pick me in their 'fantasy' Indigenous and Aboriginal sides, and there was once this rumour around that I was Tongan. To tell the honest truth, I haven't worried too much about it.

An auntie of mine did some research and she found that my great-grandfather came from North Western Ambrym in Vanuatu and my great-grandmother was from Loh Island in the Torres Strait. All we were ever told in my family was that we were Australians. My dad was born in Townsville and his dad was born in Bowen, so that makes us Australian, and we're proud of it. Dad has dark skin; his grandfather was brought here from the South Sea Islands to work in the cane-fields, which I guess is where the Tongan business comes from. Someone wrote something about it in the paper early in my career and next thing I got a phone call from some bloke asking me if I wanted to play for Tonga in the World Cup. I said, 'Mate, I'm Australian. If I ever play for anyone it'll be Australia.' That was the end of it as far as I was concerned. Unfortunately it wasn't the end of it as far as some of my team-mates at the Broncos were concerned. Wendell Sailor has called me 'The Big Tongan' ever since, which is a bit rich seeing some of his relatives got to Australia the same way as my great-grandfather. I have played in one indigenous side though, the Redfern All Blacks, who won the Aboriginal and Torres Strait Islander tournament in 1992.

That was some side. We had Choc Mundine who was about 17, Tricky Trindall who was 25, and Wes Patten who was 19. One of the sides we played against had 11 McGrady's in it, including Ewen, who won the Rothman's Medal in 1991. NSW Origin player Graham Lyons was playing for La Perouse. We beat the McGrady's side in the final. People might have read a bit into me playing in that tournament but to me it was just a chance to play some footy with my mates. You want to know my political leanings? That's it: I like to play footy with my mates, just like my dad did.

The other gun footy player in my family was my older brother Wally Junior – Little Wally, as Mum calls him. Wally was the star player in every junior rep side going. Under 10s, Under 12s, North Queensland Schoolboys, Queensland Under 15 Schoolboys, you name it, Wally was in it, usually as captain. If you'd asked anyone back then which of the Tallis boys was going to make it as a footballer, play for Queensland or even Australia, it wouldn't have been me. Even today people say to me: 'Gee, I always thought Wally would be the one . . .' It's like 'Where's Wally?' They always seem surprised that I've achieved what I have. Looking back on it, all I can tell you is that no-one is more surprised than me.

Actually, that's probably not quite true. If you had told the doctors and nurses at Townsville Base Hospital back in 1973 that Gorden Tallis would captain Australia at rugby league in 2002 they wouldn't have believed you. Matter of fact, they didn't think I'd even make it to 1974. When I was five months old I got really sick and nearly died.

JUDY TALLIS: It was Sunday. I took him to our local doctor, who thought he had a middle ear infection. The next day he was no better so I took him to a small private hospital. They took one look at him and told me to go straight to the big public hospital, where the doctors put him into isolation. They gave him all sorts of tests, a lumbar puncture, the whole bit, and said he had pneumonia and a golden staph infection. Back in those days they used to say everything was golden staph. It broke my heart to leave him there but I had to go home to the other kids. On Wednesday morning they rang me and said there was nothing they could do for him and I'd better come up to say goodbye, because he was going to die. Well, you can imagine . . . Wally had already gone to work so I called him home and we drove up to the hospital. I'll never forget it. When we walked into the ward there was this tiny little thing lying in an oxygen tent all packed in ice to try to get his temperature down. We both sat down there next to him, with the doctors and nurses saying he could die at any time. But he was a fighter, even then. He hung in there day after day, and then one day one of the ladies who worked at the hospital told me that they had held a special service at St Mary's Catholic Church and prayed for him. She put a little cross on his cot and that's when he started to get better.

I was in hospital for 12 weeks, and I still have scars on my legs from all the tests they did. Mum reckons someone was looking out for me. Like they say, God is a Queenslander.

I was the youngest of four kids. Robyn was the oldest, then there's Janitta who was two years younger. Wally was born four years later, then me two years after that. We were all close then, and we're still all close today. Mum reckons we used to fight, like all kids, but she used to say to us: 'Look after each other. You're all you've got.' Robyn used to look after Wally, and Janitta would watch out for me. Mum and Dad didn't tell them to do it, that's just how it worked out, and we probably grew up as close as any family could.

Wally and I were what you would call boisterous. Mum used to leave us at home during the school holidays when she was at work. Wally was probably about 15, I was about 13, and if we got hungry we'd just jump in Dad's car and drive down the dirt road to the shops. We'd park around the corner and go in to buy a pie or a sandwich and drive home, then hose down the car. Not that we really needed to hose it down. It was a beat up old Holden Premier, and the only time it got a wash was after me and Wally had taken it for a spin. We lived a bit out of town, over the road from this big old park. One holidays the council decided to build some soccer fields in the park, and they delivered all this topsoil. Wally and I walked over there and saw the huge piles of soil. We didn't know how it had got there but Wally decided it would look a lot better on our front lawn than in the park, so we went back and got the car. We put some plastic in the boot and spent the morning filling it up with soil and going backwards and forwards to our place. By the time Mum got home from work Wally and I had top-dressed the entire yard and were feeling pretty pleased with ourselves. Mum asked us where we had got the soil and we told her. She hit the roof. We thought we'd get some extra pocket money but I think we might have got a belting. Still, Mum never told us to take it all back and we sure had nice grass that year.

We all played sport, everything and anything we could, but the best of the lot of us was Janitta. She played netball, softball and basketball for Queensland and ran for North Queensland. Mum and Dad were the type of parents who tried to get along to every game their kids were playing in; this got to be pretty hard as we got older, especially with Mum working at the hospital on Saturdays. Some of my first memories are of going along to watch Janitta play softball. It was like a family outing. Funny thing is, it still is. Janitta's daughter Tyleisha plays softball in Brisbane and Mum is there watching with Janitta and her husband Brian every week. The rest of us get there when we can. With Janitta playing softball, my first sport was T-ball. Then Wally and I started playing basketball on Friday nights. Janitta was a top player and used to play in the indoor stadium. Wally and I were on the asphalt courts outside.

Mum used to have the problem of which one of us to watch but I soon solved that. Basketball is a frustrating game. You can't do anything. I used to play basketball back then the way I play football today – I wanted the ball and I'd go charging around the court grabbing people and diving on the ground, grazing my knees. Within five minutes I'd be sent off for having five personal fouls, so Mum would watch me for five minutes, until I got sent off, and then we'd go inside and watch Janitta. One of Janitta's team-mates in the North Queensland sides was Sandy Brondello from Sarina, which is where Wendell Sailor comes from. Sandy went on to play for Australia at the Olympics and then played professional bas-ketball in the US, and she used to stay at our place all the time. I was at a function where she was one of the guests a little while ago, and when everyone at the table was talking about Sandy's career I said 'I was a good basketball player.' She said: 'You're kidding. I used to watch you. You'd get sent off every week.' So much for my basketball career.

As soon as he was old enough, Wally started playing footy in the Under 8s. I had to wait two years before I could fol-low. Wally was a star from the moment he put on a jersey. I'd like to say I was the same, but I wasn't. Wally played five-eighth, lock or second-row – it didn't matter to him where he played, and in every team he played in he was one of the best players and usually captain. I always looked up to him, naturally enough. I remember we used to play footy games on the front lawn, between the rose bushes. He always used to let me score one try so I'd feel good – then he'd bash me. We used to play against the girls too. They were a lot bigger than us and they'd really pummel us. Their favourite tactic was the jersey swing: they'd grab us by the back of the jersey, swing us around and throw us into the garden. Mum used to sit on the front steps and be referee. She reckons she'd start off refereeing a footy game and end up refereeing a fight. After that kind of beginning I was pretty happy when I could finally play my first real game of footy against kids my own size.

My first game was for Centrals ASA at their ground in Anne Street, Aitkenvale. The only thing I remember about the game is getting changed under a tree. Dad told a reporter a couple of years ago that I scored six tries in that game. I don't know about that; I think I'd remember it if I did. Maybe I scored six tries in the season. By the time I was 12 or 13 I was hooked on rugby league. Dad used to bring *Rugby League Week* home, and when he was finished I was right into it. It was probably the only thing I'd read all week – I sure wasn't reading too many schoolbooks.

Schoolwork and me didn't mix. I think the only reason I went to primary school was to eat my lunch – and I even failed that subject because I used to swap my sandwiches with the other kids. To me, school was like driving around at night trying to find a street without a street directory. I had a lot of fun with the other kids but I never got as much out of school as I should have, and that's a real shame. These days I go to talk at schools, and the one thing I can tell the kids is that they should never be afraid of asking questions. You know how a teacher tells the class something and everyone nods their heads as if they know what he's saying and then when he walks out of the room all the quiet kids start saying to the smarter kids, 'What did he say? What did he mean?' That was me, one of the quiet kids. The funny thing is, now that I have been around for a while, I'm not afraid to ask. When Wayne Bennett tells us something before training these days it is me that the other players come up to and say, 'What did he say? What are we doing?' I just wish I'd had the confidence I have now back then. If I have one regret, it's that I didn't make more of my time at school. I spent a lot of time kicking a football down on the oval – I suppose when you look at where that got me, it wasn't all time wasted.

Once I got my hands on Dad's *Rugby League Week* I'd go straight to the section about the Brisbane comp, especially any news about Wynnum-Manly because of the North Queensland connection of Gene Miles, Greg Dowling and Colin Scott. I used to pull out the poster in the centre and stick it on my bedroom wall, no matter who it was of. I remember I had a picture of Michael O'Connor in his Australian gear above my bed and I had a picture of Wally Lewis wearing Puma boots. Needless to say, I had to have Puma boots, but while I might have had the same boots as Wally Lewis, I didn't play like him.

At that stage I was just a tall, skinny kid with straight blond hair who kicked goals and played everywhere in the side – including the wing. Yeah, that's right, the wing. When Wendell was talking about going over to rugby union at the end of the 2000 season, I gave him a pretty hard time in my newspaper column. I said that wingers were just blokes who hung around with footballers, and the only reason they score a lot of tries is because they're marked by other wingers. That summed up my early career, but I still made the Townsville side most years – probably because my name was Tallis. Also maybe because even if I didn't have all the skills, I loved the physical side of the game. I didn't care how big the other kids were, I'd try to knock them over.

One day when Dad was coaching Wally's Under 12 team they were one short, and Dad pulled me into the side even though I was two years younger.

JUDY TALLIS: I arrived from work after the game had already started and I couldn't believe it when I saw Gorden playing in the same team as Wally. I was walking towards the field and I saw Gorden running with the ball and there was this giant of a kid coming up to tackle him. I thought, 'Oh no, the big kid is going to kill my little Gorden.' I closed my eyes, and when I opened them Gorden was still running and the other boy was lying on the ground not moving. I thought, 'Oh no, my little Gorden has killed the big kid.' The fathers on the sideline used to call him 'The Kamikaze Kid'.

I remember they used to put the Townsville rep teams up in the clubhouse window and we'd all sit there waiting for them to stick it up – it was a great thrill to see your name in the

15

side. That's one thing that has never changed. Almost 20 years later, it's still great to see your name in the side.

The biggest break in my early career was when I made my first and only big junior rep side, the North Queensland Under 12s. They put me in the Townsville side for the trials as hooker. The matches were played in Burdekin and I was billeted with a local referee named Hockey Vernon. Can you believe that? Me living with a referee. One day Hockey had a barbecue and all the refs came along. I remember looking out the back yard and seeing Barry Gomersall, the Origin ref who was probably the most famous man in North Queensland at that stage. Hockey had a son named Trent who was a couple of years older than me, and we knocked around together most of the time. He had a daughter, too. Her name was Tara and she is now Mrs Wendell Sailor. Small world isn't it? When Tara and Wendell were engaged, Alfie Langer used to say things like, 'Hey Gorden, tell Wendell what you and Tara used to get up to when you were 12 and staying at her house.' To tell you the truth, we didn't get up to anything. She was just the little sister, but she was always a pretty girl, I do remember that.

When we played the trials I played hooker just like a winger. I reckon I ran the ball three times out of six from dummy half and never passed once. The selectors obviously realised I wasn't any kind of hooker, so they picked me for North Queensland as a second-rower. We played in the 1985 Country Carnival at Langlands Park in Brisbane. You know how people talk about the great junior sides and say things like, 'Oh, 1988, that was the Australian Schoolboys side that had Brad Fittler, Tim Brasher and David Fairleigh? Well I don't think anyone ever said anything like that about our Under 12 division at the Country Carnival that year. There was me, and Kenny Nagas from Bundaberg, and that was about it. And that was about it as far as my junior rep career went, too. Not like my brother Wally.

When Wally turned 17, Brian Canavan from the Broncos came knocking on our door to talk to Mum and Dad. He offered Wally a contract with the Broncos, which was like the biggest thing that could ever happen. Everyone in Queensland wanted to play for the Broncos back then, and there was Wally, just 17 years old, being given the chance. He moved to Brisbane the next year and I immediately became the world's biggest Broncos fan. You couldn't get much Broncos gear in Townsville in those days and Wally sent me up this Broncos jersey and cap. I remember mowing the lawn in them, sleeping in them, you name it. I'd love to say it all turned out perfectly for Wally, but it didn't. For a start, when he arrived in Brisbane he was just 17 years old and the Broncos didn't have an Under 21 side in those days. That meant he had to play on the Sunshine Coast, at one of the Broncos' feeder clubs. Then he played Under 19s for Redcliffe and then for Brothers, which was the Broncos' feeder club. It was all a bit of a mess, and he was a long way from home.

Robyn was working for the Broncos' sponsor, Powers Brewing, in Townsville at that time, and she organised a transfer to Brisbane so she could look after Wally. They moved into a house together. He played a few reserve grade games but then he was in a car accident. He hurt his back, and never played again. I still tell him that when my career is over we should both move back to Townsville and play for the Centrals. I can just see us, both about 100 stone, putting each other through holes.

While Wally was playing for the Broncos trying to crack the big-time, I was working my way up through the grades at Centrals. There were plenty of good young players in North Queensland then; the biggest names were probably Aaron Radeck from Townsville, David Cindric from Mt Isa and Anthony Bella from Mackay. Aaron Radeck was probably my biggest rival, not that he was too worried about me. I saw him as the benchmark. He was my age and he was getting in all the rep sides. He wasn't a huge bloke, but geez, he could hit hard. It didn't matter how big the bloke with the ball was, Aaron just loved to belt him. Wendell and I still talk about him all the time. David Cindric was a monster, the Shane Webcke of the junior rugby league. Rod Reddy once told me that Manly forward Terry Randall was so tough that 'he did weights before weights were invented'. That was David Cindric too. I was terrified of him. Anthony Bella was one of Martin Bella's brothers. There were heaps of Bellas. Anthony just happened to be the one who was my age; he was a good player too. He went down to Manly the same time I went to St George.

How did I get to St George? Well it's still a bit of a mystery to me. When I was 17 my side won the 1991 Townsville Under 18 Grand Final and I scored a few points. I think we scored 21 and I got 13 of them. Throughout the season, the coach of first grade kept asking me to sit on the bench but Mum wouldn't let me. Our top side wasn't very strong, so there was no-one to look after me against the hard heads in the other teams, such as Steve Carter. Steve was something of a legend around Townsville at that time. He'd played in Brisbane for Brothers and then St George in Sydney before heading to Townsville. He had a lot of ability but he was also a bit of a madman, getting sent off all the time. In 1986, when I was about 12, Mum took us down to Brisbane to see the Grand Final between Brothers and Wynnum at Lang Park. It was one of the biggest things that had ever happened to me. It was the first time I had ever seen a big crowd; the atmosphere was unbelievable. We had the added bonus of Townsville boy Gene Miles playing for Wynnum. I remember Steve Carter ran on for Brothers with his head shaved and the crowd all went 'ooh'. You see that sort of thing a bit these days. Back then it was pretty radical, but that was Steve Carter. At one stage of that match Geno, who was a pretty slick centre in those days, made a big bust and Steve Carter ran him down. It was pretty awesome, and the sort of thing that made every kid in Queensland want to play on Lang Park one day.

Thanks to Mum, I never got a chance to play against Steve and the other hard men of Townsville first grade. She thought I'd get hurt, and she was probably right. I'd left school after Year 10 and was working for a local builder, labouring and learning the ropes, but I still hadn't built up physically – I weighed only about 85 kilograms. Luckily – though it didn't seem too lucky at the time – the wife of the bloke I was working for got transferred out of town and he packed up and went with her, which left me without a job. We'd just won the Grand Final and my mates and I spent a few weeks celebrating. With no work and no training, I lost condition pretty fast.

About the same time, without me knowing it, Rod Reddy had rung the father of a mate of mine, asking if there were any young blokes who he should be looking at giving a trial at St George. After Rod's career at Saints had ended, he came back to Townsville as captain–coach of Centrals in 1986–87. I was 13 or 14 at the time, so I didn't exactly catch his eye then. After that he went to Barrow in England, and did pretty well over there. When Brian Smith took over at St George at the end of 1991 he brought Rod back to be reserve grade coach. Part of Rod's job was to scout new talent, so he rang a friend of his in Townsville named Geoff Aitken. I was good mates with Geoff's son Zane, and when Rod asked him if there was anyone worth having a look at, Geoff put my name on the list of three names. I don't know if the name Tallis rang a bell or what, but while the other two blokes never got a chance, out of the blue I got a call from Rod Reddy asking me if I wanted to come down to Sydney for a trial with St George. Was I surprised? This was Rod Reddy, one of the all-time greats, asking me to trial for St George, probably the most famous club in the world. Me, with no reputation, no background in rep sides and no real hope of ever playing outside Townsville.

Dad always reckoned that I used to tell Mum that I'd play for Australia one day and buy her a house and a flash car, but that was when I was eight years old. By the time I was 17 I wasn't thinking about anything like that. In those days the best young players might pay their own way down to Sydney or Brisbane for a trial, but apart from the fact that I didn't have enough money to buy a bus ticket, it just never crossed my mind that I'd be good enough. And that was despite the fact that Rod's call was the second nibble I'd had in a few weeks. After the Under 18s Grand Final win Blocker Roach had come up to our presentation night to hand out the awards, and after they showed a video of the highlights of the season he asked me if I'd like to trial with Balmain. We asked

Mum and she said I'd have to wait until after Christmas; she always felt Wally had gone to Brisbane too early. Blocker said he'd give us a call but he never did, so needless to say, when Rod asked if I was interested, I wasn't going to miss out again. I couldn't say 'yes' quickly enough.

CHAPTER TWO

DUNGEONS AND DRAGONS

The first thing I did was stop celebrating with my mates. The second thing was go for a run. I knew I had to get into some sort of shape but I didn't have much time to do it in. Two weeks later I was on a plane headed for Sydney.

Rod Reddy met me at the airport and took me to stay at his place for the week before the trial. He'd told me to bring down a video of me playing. Who did he think I was, Wally Lewis? I didn't exactly have a selection of videos of me in action, but I managed to get my hands on a film of the Under 18 Grand Final that the father of one of the players had taken. I think it was out of focus and moving up and down all the time. Most of the footage was of the bloke's son running around. When we got to Rod's place he took the video away and had a look. I think he must have been wondering what he'd got himself into. After a while he came out and said, 'We'd better go down to the park.'

I can't speak highly enough of Rod Reddy. He took me to the local park every day for a week and showed me things I'd never even heard of. I'm not knocking the coaches I'd had in Townsville, but in the junior grades they were mainly fathers, brothers or older players just helping out because no-one else would do it, and while they were doing their best, it wasn't real cutting-edge stuff. Most of the time training was just a game of touch and a bit of ball work. When Rod started showing me things it was as if he was opening my eyes for the first time. He showed me fundamentals, like hitting the ball on the advantage line and quick play-the-balls and catching the ball in front of me with two hands – all basics I never knew. I don't know whether he thought, 'Geez, this bloke's got potential' or 'Geez, this bloke needs some help', but whatever it was, I was glad he took me under his wing that week. I don't know what would have happened to me if he hadn't.

When the trial finally came I headed out to Kogarah with all my gear, just like I would have in Townsville. I didn't want to wear my Centrals uniform so I arrived in my blue Townsville shorts with a Streets ice-cream logo sewed on the side, Broncos socks that Wally had sent me, and carrying my boots in my hand. I walked into the dressing room and I've never seen so many NSW sports bags and tracksuits in my life. There were even blokes wearing stuff with Australian emblems on it. I found a quiet corner to hide in and just sat there thinking, 'What the hell am I doing here?' I was dead-set scared out of my wits. I didn't say anything to anyone and no-one said anything to me. I just remember they handed out all these different coloured jerseys to make up four teams and out we went. Someone called out my name, I went onto the field and just went off my head for 20 minutes. I fair dinkum went berserk. It might have been adrenalin brought on by fear, but I think it was more that when I was sitting in the dressing room I said to myself, 'You'll only get one chance at this, so you'd better make the most of it', and that's what I did. After 20 minutes they called us all off and sent the next teams on. Nobody had told me we were only playing 20 minutes but it was just as well, because I honestly couldn't have played 21. I was gone. I'd thrown all my eggs into one basket. Luckily, everything went right.

After the game I rang Mum and she asked how I'd gone. I told her I thought I'd gone okay and said I'd changed the way I played. The thing was, in Townsville I was a lazy player. I'd just sit back and call for the ball if I wanted it, take it up, get tackled, then sit back again. If I did eight runs and 15 tackles in a game I'd think I done pretty well. That trial I'd jammed 80 minutes of Townsville into 20 minutes at Kogarah. Brian Smith was pretty impressed. When he came up to me, the first thing he said to me was: 'Well, son, you know the best thing ever to come out of Queensland is the Pacific Highway.' After a while I realised that was just what he was like. He had this funny sense of humour, and he used to say things that if you didn't know he was joking, you could take the wrong way. I remember he said to Lance Thompson when he first came to the club: 'Listen here, son, there's only been two red-headed players and one of them wasn't even

that good, so the odds are against you.' During those trials
he stood in front of us all and said: 'Okay fellas, there're
60 kids here and probably only one of you will ever make it to
first grade, so could that bloke please put up his hand so the
rest of you can go home and stop wasting my time.' Like I
said, he was a funny bloke, but he took a while to get used to.

After another week training down at the park with Rod,
they gave me a couple more runs on the weekend. I made the
cut and then they talked to Mum and Dad and offered me a
scholarship.

*ROD REDDY: I remembered him from Townsville as a 13 or 14-
year-old when I was captain–coach of Centrals. He was the little
brother; it was his big brother Wally who was the star. Back then
Gordie was like a puppy dog, all full of energy. You'd let him off
the lead and he'd run around all day, and when it was time to go
home you'd put him back on the lead.*

*When I got back from coaching overseas I was thinking about
kids I might be able to bring down to Sydney and I got out the old
programs from Townsville and saw his name. I wondered what had
happened to him and gave Geoff Aitken a call. Geoff gave me three
names. The other blokes didn't get a run because I just didn't think
they were good enough, but I remembered all that energy Gorden
had and had a hunch.*

*He brought a tape down with him and you could see the poten-
tial was there, but geez he was raw. He got so far back to run onto
the ball that I thought he was a fast bowler coming in off the
sightscreen. I took him down to the park and started teaching him*

the basics. Just little things that Harry Bath and Billy Smith had taught me when I came down from North Queensland. Not much has changed since then. The field's still the same size, it's still 13 blokes playing 13 and you play the ball the same way. People just tend to gloss over the little things.

It was simple stuff, basics like not wasting energy by getting too deep, taking short footsteps, catching the ball going towards it . . . nothing magic, but Gorden picked it up pretty quick. We gave him a run the first week and he went well. The second week Brian Smith dragged him off after about six minutes. Gorden was saying, 'What did I do wrong?' He hadn't done anything wrong, he'd done great – we just didn't want anyone else to see him before we could sign him.

I guess it's nice of him to say I helped him along the way, but the truth is I just showed him a few basics. You can't coach what Gorden Tallis has got under his shirt. You have to be born with it.

They said they'd bring me down to play Under 19s and pay me $3000 for the season. I couldn't believe it. I would have played for $3, but $3000? That would have been enough to make me the top paid player in Townsville. They said they'd either pay it to me or put it towards my rent and I told them to pay my rent so I wouldn't have to worry about it. It meant I never actually saw any money, but I wasn't complaining. A couple of months earlier I was an Under 18 player sitting around drinking beer with my mates. Now I was a professional footballer with the mighty St George Dragons; it was like a dream.

After I signed I went back to Townsville for Christmas and I really threw myself into the training, running around the roads and doing sit-ups and all that. I knew I'd been out of condition when I went down the first time and I could see how fit some of the players were in Sydney so I got stuck into it. I've never been what you would call a keen trainer. I'm not one of those blokes who loves to run, but I'll always do what has to be done, which is what I did then, for hours every day.

WAYNE BENNETT: First time I met him was in Townsville just before he came down to St George. We had his brother Wally at the Broncos but I didn't know Gorden from a bar of soap. I was up there for the Gene Miles–Greg Dowling Testimonial and he's walked up to me and said: 'I'm Gorden Tallis and you've got the wrong Tallis down there. I'm going down to St George and I'm going to make it.' I just looked at him and said, 'Well good luck, mate.'

Townsville at Christmas is like a sauna, so the weight just fell off me, and by the time the family was waving me off at the airport to go back to Sydney I was like a whippet. Saying goodbye to Mum that day was one of the hardest things I've ever done. It was pretty emotional. She was crying, I was crying and I don't think I stopped until we were coming in to land in Sydney. But if I was feeling bad then, things were about to get worse. Brian Smith was there to pick me up and he took one look at me and said: 'What's happened to you?' He was expecting to see this big second-rower who'd played in the trials, but after all the training I'd done in the heat of Townsville here I was all of 86 kilograms. I told him I'd been sick.

BRIAN SMITH: He was very raw when we first saw him but we liked what we saw. He was so strong, so physical, even as a kid. Somehow they didn't have much of an opinion of him back in north Queensland. At that time it seemed like every kid in Queensland got a junior state jumper because then if they were signed by a Sydney club the Queensland Rugby League could claim a full transfer fee. I think Gorden was one of only about six or seven kids aged over 15 in Queensland who hadn't played for the State.

I remember soon after we signed him I went to Townsville for a coaching clinic. Gorden wasn't involved but he came along to see some of his mates and he and I had a bit of a chat. After he walked off, a couple of the local coaches asked me what I was talking to him for. I told them we had just signed him. Their reaction, expletives deleted, was: 'You're kidding. He can't play.' It seems incredible now, but they just didn't rate him. Not that it worried him. I heard after his brother Wally went to the Broncos, Gorden told Wayne Bennett that they'd signed the wrong Tallis. That typifies Gorden. He would never have meant to put his brother down. It was just an honest appraisal of the situation as he saw it.

The club put me in this house with five other young players – Nathan Brown, Matthew Parsons, Scott Park, Scott Ingram and Paul Sanderson. Luke Felsch was billeted with a family around the corner but he stayed at our place freeloading on the couch every weekend, so you could say there were seven of us. What was pretty unusual was that every one of us went on to play first grade either at Saints or some other club, which threw Brian Smith's one in 60 theory out the window. Actually, that wasn't the only thing we threw out the window. By the time I moved out a year and a half later that poor old house was a complete wreck. If you wanted to walk in the front door you had to lift it up and rest it against the wall. It was a pigsty, but gee we had a good time in it. It was right behind the leagues club and it was like a halfway house for all the Under 19 and Under 21 players before and after training. The best thing that ever happened to us was when they opened a Sizzlers restaurant in the leagues club car park. That was the day our stove got turned off for good, except for when Mum came to stay.

JUDY TALLIS: The first time I came to stay he picked me up at the airport and brought me back to the house. It was such a mess. He took me into his room and it was so tiny we could hardly both fit in. I said to him, 'Where am I going to sleep, Gorden?' and he said, 'Right here. You get the bed, Mum. I'll sleep on the floor.' He was so proud to be down there living on his own. I don't think those boys ever cooked a meal. When I was down there I'd cook up big roasts and plenty of vegetables so they'd get some decent food into

them but I think when I walked out the door that stove didn't get
turned on again until the next time I came to stay.

The Sizzlers used to have an all-you-can-eat buffet, and man,
did we eat a lot. I don't know how they broke even. We'd eat
there every night.

Nathan Brown and I got to be real close mates – still are
today – and the rest of us all got along well too, but when I
first arrived I have to admit I felt like packing up and going
straight back to Townsville. What happened was that I was
the first to arrive. Apart from those two weeks at Rod
Reddy's place, I'd never been out of Townsville in my life and
Brian Smith just dropped me at the house and said, 'See you
at training next week.' For four days I was on my own in an
empty house in a strange city without two coins to rub
together. I didn't even have a TV, and for a bloke like me
who loves to be around people, it was like being in jail. When
Scott Park finally walked through the front door with all his
gear I nearly hugged him. Then little by little the others
started arriving and pretty soon it was party time.

GEOFF CARR (former St George chief executive): That was a
great bunch of kids we had in that house. We had a bloke named
Max Ninnis in charge of scouting our junior players back then. He
is still with Saints, which gives you an idea of his ability – he has

survived all those coaches. Max is one of those people who mightn't make a great coach himself, but he has great knowledge. He's a great judge of ability. Rod Reddy had brought Gorden down and Max had scouted the others. I used to play football with Nathan Brown's dad John, and John used to spot players for us.

One time he told us he was sending a kid down for a trial and he said he'd send his son Nathan along to keep this kid company. We gave Nathan a run and Brian Smith rang John the next day and said, 'Forget the other kid, why didn't you tell us about Nathan?' He was the best player in the trial. So around that time we managed to get a great group of young players to the club. We put a lot of them together in that house. I hate to think what went on there but I do know Gorden was famous for driving all the others mad.

The club got me and Andrew Walker, who had just come over from Randwick Rugby Union Club, jobs on Hurstville Council. I think Andrew used up all his sick days in the first month. My first job was whipper-snippering grass along the side of the roads. At the end of the week they gave me $350 take-home pay – an absolute fortune. I was over the moon. Our boss was Billy Smith's brother, Alex, so we were what they called Koala Bears – a protected species. That's not to say I didn't get stuck into the work. I loved it. I was there for two years until I made first grade and couldn't fit work around my training any more. When I go down to Sydney to play these days, if I have any spare time I try to get over to the depot to say g'day to the boys, and whenever I go past it

I always check out this garden bed I made. It's a beauty. Mum's sick of me pointing it out to her whenever she's with me. 'Isn't that a great garden bed, Mum?' I'll say and she'll say, 'Yes, love, it's beautiful.' It's not everyone who can drive along a public road and see something he's built.

That first year we played Under 19 Jersey Flegg on Saturdays. There were only ten games per season, so if we weren't standing by for Under 21s we were supposed to play for local Under 19 sides on Sundays. One week, seven of us played for Hurstville United, the worst team in the competition. They hadn't won a game for two years and they were up against the gun side in the competition. We hammered that gun side and won easily, so they complained to the club. The club had to split us up then, which stopped the fun a bit. After that, most of the time the club doctor would just say we were injured after our Flegg matches so we didn't have to play on the Sundays. That suited me, because we liked to have a beer after the games on Saturday nights and try to chat up Brownie's leftovers. It turned out to be a great year. I wouldn't have changed a thing. Of course I would have loved to play for the Broncos, but they didn't have the same Under 19 and Under 21 set-up as the Sydney clubs, and after what happened with Wally I don't know if it would have worked out as well for me there as it did in Sydney. As it was, for the first time in my life I started to get picked in the top rep sides; the difference was that it was for Sydney and NSW teams instead of Brisbane or Queensland.

The first side I was chosen for was City Under 19. All I had to do was get through our Jersey Flegg match against Manly the week before in one piece. Easier said than done. Anthony Bella was playing for Manly and there was a bit of rivalry between the two North Queensland boys, so when he got the ball I really tried to belt him – and smashed my thumb on his head. When we were driving home I got the boys to drop in at a 24-hour medical centre for an X-ray, and sure enough, the thumb was broken. The next day I asked our club doctor, Martin Raftery, who is now the doctor for the Wallabies, if there was any chance I could play for City the next week. I was dead keen to get on the field and asked if there was any more damage I could do. He had a look and told me I probably couldn't make it any worse and he'd ask the City doctor Nathan Gibbs to give me a painkilling injection before the match. With that good news I headed off to City training – and managed not to catch a ball all week. Dr Gibbs gave me the jab before the game and it went perfectly. We beat the Country boys 76–nil and I played pretty well, without any problems from my thumb. I couldn't feel a thing all game, but as soon as it wore off it hurt like hell. I wasn't too worried though, because after the match they named the NSW Under 19 side to take on Queensland. It was like waiting for the Townsville under age sides all over again. When the team was announced, my name was in it. It was incredible. Here I was, less than a year away from Townsville, being named in a NSW team. The fact that my first major rep match would be in a blue jersey rather than a maroon one didn't worry me one bit. Just the opposite, actually, because Aaron Radeck and David Cindric, a couple of North Queensland boys who had always been chosen for the junior rep teams ahead of me, were named in the Queensland side, so I figured I had something to prove. There was one little problem to get past before that happened, though – my broken thumb.

Luckily, there was a six-week gap between the City game

and the interstate match, so I could go straight into plaster. The main thing was not letting the NSW officials know there was a problem with me, because if they did, they would pull me straight out of the side. Obviously I couldn't play for the St George Flegg team, so I trained with first grade for the six weeks. After my name hadn't appeared in the program for a few weeks one of the NSW managers rang Brian Smith to see if there was anything wrong with me. 'Anything wrong with Gorden?' Brian said, 'No, of course not, he's training the house down. It's just that he's too valuable to play in Flegg. We're saving him for the Under 21 semi-finals.' They bought it, and I got the plaster taken off a couple of days before the match.

I was one of only two Flegg players chosen in the side – Nik Kosef was the other. The rest of the team were reserve grade or Under 21 players like Rodney Howe, John Hopoate and Kenny Nagas or first-graders like Luke Ricketson. It was a hot side, and we won 26–12. It's funny when you think how I've come to hate that blue jersey now, but on that day I was just happy to have done my bit to beat the Maroons. Things would change within a very short time.

After the interstate game the selectors chose an Australian Under 19 side to play against the Australian Schoolboys and once again I had the buzz of seeing my name in the team list. It was a funny sort of game, more a tune-up match for the schoolboys who were about to go on tour than a fair dinkum rep match, and a lot of the clubs wouldn't let their players take part. I went and asked Brian Smith if I could play and he couldn't stop himself getting in one of those funny digs of his. 'Yeah,' he said, 'you can play. It's always a great honour to play for Australia and you'll probably never get another chance.' At half-time during the match I wasn't so sure if he'd done me a favour – we were down 22–nil. But we came back to lose just 24–22 in what was a pretty entertaining match.

By then the Flegg season had ended and I moved into grade footy. It had been a great season for me so far and I was really finding my feet, not just with my football but in Sydney and the club environment generally. After starting off as a shy country boy who cried on the plane down from Townsville, my real personality was starting to come through. When I first moved into the house I wouldn't say boo to a goose; I was just some blow-in from Queensland trying to get a start in the Flegg side. But after a while I turned into what Brownie called 'a cheeky Murri from Townsville'.

NATHAN BROWN: I knew the Under 21 players, and they used to come to the house all the time before training. They'd sit around watching TV, maybe get a drink or something to eat out of the fridge. It didn't worry me but it started to bug Gordie. Finally he had a go at them. He marched in, looked at them sitting there and said: 'Who do you blokes think you are? Haven't you got a bloody house of your own? Just because you play Under 21s you think you're something special. Anyway I'll be playing in your side soon.' They were all like: 'Yeah sure, dickhead', but when they started coming down to a few of our matches and saw him smashing blokes and getting in the rep sides they were all trying to be his mates. It was, 'Hey Gordie, how ya going, Gordie?'

As it turned out, I did get into the same team as those blokes, and a lot of them became my mates. When the Flegg season ended I played four Under 21 matches. It was a real step up. Just like when I'd come from Queensland for the trial, the pace of the game found me out. I found the hits were a lot harder and the speed was greater and I had to do a fair bit of work to catch up. After four games in Under 21s I went to reserves, and that was another step up. I had four games in reserves, but because they couldn't make the semi-finals the selectors dropped me back down so I would be eligible for the Under 21 semis. The gun sides in the Under 21s were us and Wests. We finished second behind them in the minor premiership even though we beat them in the last match of the season at Kogarah. That day Brian put me on in first grade for the first time.

I'd like to say it was one of the great first grade debuts of all time, but in fact I had a shocker. I went on at half-time, dropped the ball cold twice, got thumped the first time I took it up and generally didn't know what was going on. Wests were a good side then. They were coached by Warren Ryan and had players like Terry Hill, Jim Dymock, Paul Langmack, Cement Gillespie, Darren Britt and Joey Thomas. Thinking back on it now, the whole thing was a blur. The pace of the game got to me, the occasion got to me, everything got to me. One thing I do remember is that Graeme Wynn, who had gone over to Wests after a long career at Saints, was chewing gum. At one stage I went down the short side and got tackled by Andrew Farrar and Wynn came over the top and pushed my head into the ground like no-one had ever done to me in my life. I was the new kid then so I just copped it. When I got up I reckon I had half of

Kogarah Oval hanging off the side of my face. After 20 minutes Brian sent the hook out and replaced me.

As debuts go, it wasn't a world beater, but as far as giving me a taste of what first grade football was all about it was invaluable, and I have to thank Brian Smith for bringing me along the way he did. In years to come Brian and I would have our clashes, but back then he couldn't have been better to me. When I look back on my career, I give him and Rod Reddy full credit. I wouldn't have been the player I am today if I hadn't gone down to Sydney and that wouldn't have happened if it wasn't for Brian and Rod. I owe them both a lot.

BRIAN SMITH: There was one thing about Gorden which impressed me so much that I still point it out to young players today and that was the way he approached training. He didn't do it every time but I can still see him running out on to Kogarah Oval for training and I'm sure that in his head he could hear the crowd cheering. He would get himself in a state where he would practise as if he was playing a real game. Because it was a bit foreign some of the senior players thought he was quite loopy but since then I've been to the US and seen NFL players doing the same thing. They will be training unopposed but they'll run and twist and take off as if there is someone chasing them. Gorden was the same. There would be no-one in front of him but he would push off and accelerate as if he was trying to beat the cover defence. He had that ability to capture the emotion of the game situation in his mind. That is why he had such an impact as an interchange player. Some blokes fall asleep on the bench or just sit there enjoying the game. Not

Gorden. It is almost as if he is out there playing and when he actually gets on to the field he is ready to go. Even as a youngster he had this awesome ability to jump straight into the game.

The regular season ended with two Grand Final losses for Saints. I played in the Under 21s and we lost to Wests by a point after having beaten them in the major semi. I scored a try, got involved in an all-in brawl and spent 10 minutes in the sin-bin, then sat and watched the Broncos beat our first grade to take out their first premiership. They were an awesome side then. Even though I played for Saints, I had to admire the way they played the game. Blokes like Alfie Langer, Kevvie Walters, Steve Renouf, Mick Hancock and Willie Carne – and that forward pack with Glenn Lazarus, Kerrod Walters, Trevor Gillmeister, Alan Cann and Terry Matterson. Saints went out thinking they had a chance, but the truth was that the Broncos that year were in a class of their own. You could only shake your head and watch in awe.

There was still one very special game for me before my fairytale first year came to a close. Saints were headed to Bali for their end of year trip, and even though I wasn't eligible to go, I was pretty interested in the match they were playing along the way. The first stop on the trip was Townsville, where the Grand Final team had arranged to play the local rep side to make a bit of money to put on the bar in Bali. When I heard that, I knew I had to be involved. Brownie and I went to Mark Coyne, the trip organiser, and I begged him to let me play. We said we'd pay our own way. Coynie knew how much it meant to me and said the club would pay for us to go to Townsville and he'd give us a run at some stage. The 'some stage' turned out to be most of the game, because a couple of the players were in no state to play footy. A few of them were as full as a state school on the plane trip from Sydney and a couple more were still drinking in the casino on the afternoon of the match, so I think Mark was pretty glad he'd taken us along. To me it was the perfect end to the year. Here I was, 12 months after playing in the Townsville Under 18 Grand Final, running back out onto the same field with the St George side which had just played in the Sydney Grand Final, alongside blokes like Dave Barnhill, Scott Gourley, Mark Coyne and Mick Potter. Mum and Dad and my sisters and all my mates were in the crowd. As we walked off after the match I remember putting my arm around Nathan Brown's shoulder and saying, 'Pinch me Brownie, I've got to be dreaming.' And that was only the start.

CHAPTER THREE

SAINTS AND SINNERS

That 20 minutes of first grade Brian gave me at the end of 1992 was like a sip of beer on a hot afternoon. I was 19 years old, I'd had a taste, and I wanted more.

When we got back together after the first-graders had been to Bali it became pretty obvious that I had moved up in the ranks as far as the coaches were concerned. I was moved up to reserve grade and Brian gave me a lot of time off the interchange bench in firsts. That suited me down to the ground. I would have liked to be a starter in firsts, but Saints had some great back-rowers and I was just happy to be among the likes of Wally Fullerton-Smith, David Barnhill,

Scott Gourley, Brad Mackay, Jeff Hardy, Matt Elliott, Shane
Walker and Jeremy Donougher. Plus the reserve grade coach
was Rod Reddy, and I was still learning heaps from him and
Brian. In years to come Wayne Bennett would put the finishing touches on my game, but being able to learn from
people like Rod, who was one of the best back-rowers of all
time, and Brian, who is a very smart coach, is an opportunity
you don't pass up.

I've always found it hard to give myself a rap, but I'd have
to say that my game really started to improve in 1993. I
played first grade in the Charity Shield against Souths in the
pre-season, and by the time I played reserve grade against
Canberra early in the season I was going okay.

*CRAIG BELLAMY: I was Canberra Under 21 coach in 1993.
Saints always used to play one home game in Adelaide back then,
and that year it just happened to be against Canberra. The lower
grades still played in Sydney, so my team played as the curtain-
raiser to the reserve grade side at Kogarah. I'd heard about Gorden
but never seen him, and I was interested to see how he went.*

*I can honestly say I have never seen one player at any level –
from the bush up to playing for Australia – physically dominate a
game the way he did that day. Dean Lance was coaching the Canberra reserve grade side and we still talk about it. I remember us
just standing there watching and saying, 'How good is this bloke?'*

*The thing was, he was only about 19 years old, and in those days
reserve grade sides were stacked with experienced, hard men. Every
time he had the ball he'd make 20 metres or more. He was literally*

picking up blokes and throwing them out of the way when they tried to tackle him. I'm not kidding when I say he ran over the top of our blokes – they had stud marks on their chests in the dressing room after the game. Our poor little halves, he terrorised them.

You talk about a player taking over a game . . . well I've seen halfbacks do it with guile, but I've never seen anyone do it with sheer power and aggression like that, before or since.

I got to know him when I was assistant coach at Brisbane of course. My only experience of him up to then was this bloke who would monster opposition sides on the field, but when I arrived I saw the other side of him. I was in an apartment for a few weeks before my family arrived. I didn't know anyone in town and he just took it upon himself to look after me. He'd drop around a couple of times a week and we'd go out for a feed. He's got a heart of gold. He'd do anything for you, but seeing him on the field that day in 1993 you wouldn't know it. He can still do things like that when he sees the white line and has one of those days, but I still think that was the most dominant game he ever played.

After that Brian started using me more off the bench and management called me in to upgrade my contract. Up until then I still hadn't seen any money. Everything I earned – all $3000 of it – went to pay my rent, but a few games into the season they offered me $9000 a year for two years. Considering where I had come from in such a short time, this was a fortune. I signed on the dotted line and went out and bought a home unit – I thought I'd better do it before the house fell down around our ears.

We were still all having a great time together. The club was really close, because in those days it was still a real old-fashioned club with three grades, unlike now, and at St George everyone trained together two nights a week. That meant it didn't matter what grade you were in, you knew everyone and everyone knew you. Even in my first season, although I'd usually hang around with the other Under 19s, I'd still have a beer with a bloke like David Barnhill back at the club after a home game. In 1993 I felt a lot more confident, and because I was part of the first grade squad, I got to know everyone a lot better. Having had two sides in the 1992 Grand Finals and being up at the top of the table for most of 1993, it was a very happy club, as most successful clubs are. Everyone worked hard and enjoyed the results but there were also plenty of laughs.

There were also two pests: Nathan Brown and Noel Goldthorpe. They were two of the smallest blokes in the club, but just like the little blokes at the Broncos, Alfie Langer and Kevvie Walters, they made the most noise. They loved the practical jokes. They put itching powder in my tracksuit pants for weeks before I cottoned on. They thought it was funny; I wanted to kill them. Because we trained and played at Kogarah, we used to leave our boots in the dressing room between sessions and matches. That was at the start of the health kick, when players used to eat fruit immediately after a game or training session instead of throwing down a few beers. Well some players used to eat it; others, namely Brown and Goldthorpe, used to hide it, then stick it in your boots before they left. Week after week we'd arrive at the dressing room and stick our feet in our boots to find rotten bananas or strawberries jammed inside. Still, that was better than what Goldie did to Wayne Bartrim. One day he put prawn shells in his hubcaps. Wayne couldn't work out what the smell was and had to drive around with the windows open and his head halfway out of the car, in the fresh air. There was something about cars which excited those two. At the time the club was sponsored by Newman's Mitsubishi and everyone was driving identical Magnas. All the keys for the ignition and burglar alarms looked exactly the same. When Brownie and Goldie weren't putting itching powder in your jocks or fruit in your boots, they were sneaking into everyone's gear and swapping the car keys around. The identical keys would fit into the ignition but they wouldn't start the car, and when the burglar alarm started up you couldn't switch it off. Hilarious – as long as it didn't happen to you. One of the only blokes who didn't have a Mitsubishi Magna was our winger, Mark 'The Javelin' Bell. Mark was one of those blokes who had a short fuse and would blow up about things, which was like a red rag to Brownie and Goldie. Mark's pride and joy was his Ford Laser, so they put an ad in the *Trading Post* offering it for sale at a ridiculously low price. Then they put his phone number and added the words: 'Shift worker. Call only after 11.30 pm.' He was getting calls all night. Everyone thought it was pretty funny. Everyone except The Javelin.

Probably the most embarrassing moment of my life happened that year – when Brownie 'pantsed' me at Sizzlers. Pantsing was all the rage back then. I think it started out at Penrith. Freddie Fittler told me that Mark Geyer was a master at it. The idea was to walk up behind someone when they least expected it – preferably when they had their hands full – and pull their pants right down to their ankles. MG did it to Freddie when he was handing out the awards at a juniors presentation day and another time when the Panthers were at a shopping centre promotion. Freddie was on the big stage waving to a couple of thousand shoppers when MG came up behind him and whooshka. Trouble was, Freddie wasn't wearing undies. He did it to Greg Alexander the night the Panthers won the premiership. Brandy was on the stage leading everyone in the club in a rendition of that Boom Crash Opera song 'Hands in the Air'. He had his hands in the air all right and it was an opportunity too good to miss for MG. Which is probably what Brownie thought when I was standing in line waiting to get a table at Sizzlers that night. The place was packed and we were out near the front counter, with a giant glass wall behind us. I think I was wearing a pair of Brownie's shorts – we weren't real big on washing our clothes those days – and just like Freddie at that shopping centre, I wasn't wearing any Reg Grundies. Brownie pantsed me and I panicked. Somehow I got the shorts tangled up around my ankles and couldn't get them up. All the people who were walking past outside and looking in to see how crowded the place was got a full view of me bending over and everyone inside looked up to see why Brownie was laughing. I finally got the pants up and took off after Brownie, who ran into the restaurant with me in hot pursuit. I was so embarrassed I thought I could never go into that place again, but hunger got the better of me and we were back the next night.

While we were all having good fun off the field, I was having a lot of fun on the field as well. Brownie and I were pretty thick, Choc Mundine was around, and Jason Stevens was about the same age as me. We all formed a bit of a gang, enjoying our footy and starting to get a taste of the big-time. For the first half of the season I'd play reserve grade and sit on the bench for firsts with Brian maybe giving me ten minutes late in the game. Then one Sunday morning I got a call from Brian telling me to get to the ground at 1.30 pm instead of 10.30 am.

It was the morning after the City–Country game, and Barnhill and Gourley had both pulled up sore, so I was in the starting line-up for the first time. Guess who the game was against? You got it in one: the Broncos. I remember I was pretty nervous all morning. It's hard enough starting in first grade for the first time without it being against the gun team in the competition. As I said earlier, Brisbane had an aura around them, and while I might have preferred running on against one of the lesser teams first up, you have to go into the deep end at some stage, and this was as good a time as any. Just like the first time I got on in first grade the year before, it wasn't exactly one for the scrapbooks. They flogged us, but my own performance was okay. After that I started to get more of a go in first grade.

It was around then that the media started to notice me and give me a bit of coverage, but even if I was the type of bloke who would get a swelled head, my family made sure I kept my feet firmly on the ground. The first time I had my picture in the paper was when they did a story about me in *Rugby League Week*. It was titled 'Doing The Hard Yards' and had a photo of me in my council worker's gear of King Gee shirt and shorts, holding a shovel and standing beside a council truck. I was so excited, I rang up Mum and told her, 'Quick, go out and get *Rugby League Week*, I'm in it.' She went out and bought it and I rang her up to see what she thought of seeing her son in the paper. 'Gee, love,' she said. 'You could have ironed your shirt, couldn't you?'

I'd be lying if I said it isn't a thrill to see yourself in the paper for the first time. After all, that's what you dream about when you are a kid. Just like I used to read about players in *Rugby League Week* and put their pictures on my bedroom wall, I hoped that one day I'd be the one whose poster was on some kid's wall. But much as any player likes to start getting recognition in the press, it is the recognition of other players that you really want. Getting my picture in the paper for the first time was good, but it was nothing compared to hearing my name shouted out by an opposition player. The first time you hear an opponent yell out to his team-mates, 'Tallis is on, Tallis is on' when you come into the game off the bench you know you have arrived. An opposition coach has thought you are important enough to include in his game plan, and that's a great feeling. You have to take it as a compliment, but it also makes your job harder, because you can't get away with the things you used to when you were an unknown. Still, that's what the game is all about. Letting people know who you are and challenging them to try to stop you playing the way you want to.

The first thing you want to do when you make first grade is test yourself against the players you really respect. Mal Meninga was the biggest name in the game when I started, but there wasn't much chance that Mal and I would ever go one-on-one. I was more interested in seeing how I lined up against the big name back-rowers like Brad Clyde or Paul Sironen, or the hard men like Les Davidson and Ian Roberts. Davidson and Roberts were two of the toughest men I have ever seen on the field, and they were the ones who set the benchmark as far as I was concerned.

The thing I really liked about Les Davidson was that there

was no garbage in his game. He was just a very hard man who played the game straight up and down. He put everything into every hit-up and tackle, and if you took him on, you had to be prepared to cop plenty. I remember one time we played a trial match against Cronulla and Les was standing over Brad Mackay in the play-the-ball. Brad pushed him and Les let go with a right hand that couldn't have travelled more than six inches. Brad went down just as Wayne Collins tried to jump in and stop the punch. And bang, Les cleaned Wayne up in the follow through. Two blokes out cold from the one punch.

Ian Roberts was another one who could hold his hands up – Johnny Lewis used to take the players for boxing training on the 1994 Kangaroo tour and he reckoned Robbo could have been a champion. But like Les, he could hurt you just as much with a legitimate hard hit. One time, when we were still in the Under 19s, the boys from the household went to see a game at Brookvale Oval, Manly versus Canberra. Roberts only played about 30 minutes, but in one passage of play he flew out of the line twice and smashed Brent Todd and Gary Coyne with consecutive tackles. They both went off on stretchers.

I was watching a game on the 1994 Kangaroo tour on TV when Ian belted some bloke. He did something I'd never seen a footballer do – he went for the body. He hit the bloke in the head a couple of times, and when the bloke covered up Ian went downstairs: one-two in the guts. The bloke went straight down. It was like being ringside at a Mike Tyson fight. Everyone was a little afraid of Ian back then. There were rumours he was gay but he hadn't really come out, and you just weren't sure how to behave around him, especially when he'd belted a couple of blokes on the field who'd had a go at him about being gay. I remember one time Wendell and I were doing a Super League ad with him. The two of us were having lunch together and Wendell picked up a banana and started going, 'Oh Ian, oh Ian.' Just then Roberts came in and started walking towards us. I could see him but Wendell had his back to him. Being a good mate I didn't say anything to Wendell and he was still going, 'Ian, oh Ian.' Robbo walked up, put his hand on Wendell's shoulder and whispered, 'Enjoying yourself, Wendell?' You couldn't really say Wendell has ever gone pale, but I reckon he came close that day.

Davidson, Roberts and Cement Gillespie were the types of player I grew up watching, and they were the ones I respected. That's why I would always challenge myself to see how I went against them. I wouldn't be stupid enough to run straight at them, but just playing on the same field as them would give me a huge buzz. What I really wanted was for them to notice me. I'd go up to them after the game and shake hands. Usually with other players I would be like, 'Thanks for the game.' With them it was more, 'Pleased to meet you.' I guess I was always hoping one of them would say, 'Well played, good game.' I don't think they ever did, but you can't blame a kid for trying.

I'm not sure if they ever put a little extra into the tackles when they got their hands on me, but I like to think they did. That would mean I was getting somewhere. I know I always try that little bit harder when I've caught up with one of the up and comers these days. In the early days of my career there were a lot of good young back-rowers coming through, such as Steve Menzies, Nik Kosef and Daniel Gartner, and

I'm sure the old hardheads were looking at them very carefully. These days when I play against a Nathan Hindmarsh or before that, a Bryan Fletcher, I always try to let them know I'm still around. There are plenty of good young backrowers coming up now, but the one that I really admire most is Ali Laviti'iti from the Warriors. He's got footwork that many backs envy and unbelievable ball skills. He is the type of player I love to watch.

As the 1993 season went on, Brian used me more and more as a tactical weapon. That's when the press picked up on it and the 'Raging Bull' business started. The good thing, as far as I was concerned, was that I knew exactly when I would be used and for how long. That way I could give it everything I had. I would go on for the last 15 minutes of the first half and half-time couldn't come soon enough. You've got to remember, I was still young and physically raw. If Brian hadn't used me the way he did, I'd have burned myself out early in the game and be no good to anyone. Players use up a lot of energy in the first 20 minutes of a game; the difference is that everyone starts off fresh then. I would go on right when the intensity was dropping off and blokes were struggling to get their second wind. It was the same in the second half when I went on: the game had slowed down. Deep down I would have liked to start the game – everyone wants to run on – but the truth is I probably wasn't up to it. When I think of the way I played 80 minutes in the 2000 Origin match at full intensity, I know that I would have had a better chance of winning Gold Lotto than doing that in 1993.

I suppose in that respect I was having a dream run. Because I was on for short bursts I was really getting noticed. In a small way it was like Mark Riddell, the kicker at Saints who sticks his arm up when he moves in for a shot at goal. The crowd knows what is going to happen and they look forward to it. When Mark sticks his arm up, so do the St George supporters. And while I didn't do anything fancy like that, the Saints fans used to know I'd be on after 20 minutes and they'd give me a bit of a cheer. It was the same at other grounds; when I stood up to take off my tracksuit, they'd start yelling at me. I really like it when the crowd gets into it. I don't care whether they are cheering or booing, as long as they are involved. They have paid their money for a seat and I'd much rather see them enjoying themselves and feeling part of the action than sitting there quietly. Some crowds are better than others, of course. I usually cop a pretty hard time when we play in Newcastle, but that's fine by me. And Origin is something else again. Most of the time I can't hear what is actually being said, but when everyone in the crowd is excited the adrenalin spills over the fence and really gets me going too. Sometimes, if there's a break in play or I'm waiting for the kick-off, I might hear someone scream something at me or call me a name and I'll turn and give them a smile, but generally I'm too involved to interact with them. There have been a couple of notable exceptions which I'll go into later, but they are pretty rare. Generally, as long as people don't throw things onto the field or hold up rude signs, I'm fine. Cheer, boo, do whatever you want. It's your money.

It was the same away from the field that year as well. For the first time, I started to get recognised when I went out. Now that's a really weird feeling. First off you think there's something wrong, like your fly is open or something. Then you realise that people are staring at you because they know who you are. I started to get asked to go onto *The Footy Show* that year and do silly things – once they body-painted me in a St George jumper that Mum had to get off with nail polish remover – and the papers started doing more stories about me and calling me the 'super-sub', so I suppose my face was getting better known. Again, just like with the booing and shouting from the grandstands, I don't have a worry with that, it just takes a bit of getting used to.

I'm lucky that it has never been a real problem. I always go back to the club after every home game and I like saying hello to the fans. If they ever start going on about what is wrong with the team or how we should be doing things differently, I just point to Wayne Bennett and say, 'I think the coach would be very interested in that, mate; no-one listens to me.'

WAYNE BENNETT: Off the field? What do you want me to talk about – his generosity, his humility? I've seen it time and time again. If a kid's a battler, if someone needs something, he'll give the shirt off his back. He's kind-hearted, as generous as buggery, and he sticks up for the underdog. He'll always test the bully.

Mostly I just get blokes hanging out of cars and yelling out 'G'day, Gordie' and stuff like that. I don't know if I'd cop it as well if I was one of the real big name players. I saw the way Wally Lewis was followed around during Origin, and one time I had to do a promotion with Shane Warne. He had to have a couple of bodyguards to keep people away from him. I suppose when you get to that stage it is more than being a sportsman. He is a celebrity, and that is another thing altogether. I really can't imagine living that way. Even with me, people come up at the worst times and try to have a yarn.

I try to talk to everyone, but sometimes it is impossible to share your time. I remember being at a pub for my brother Wally's buck's night when a stranger walked up and started talking to me, which was fine. Then another bloke came up and tried to pull me away. I said to him, 'Mate, I'm just talking to this bloke here', and he went right off. He said, 'Geez, I just wanted five minutes of your time.' I said, 'Well, right now I'm giving this bloke five minutes of my time' but he was still dirty. The same thing happened when I was with my wife Christine in Townsville recently. We were waiting in a line for a cab and the bloke in front was talking to me, the bloke behind was talking to me and another bloke walked up the road to speak to me. I tried to juggle all three but the third bloke got angry and stormed off when I was listening to what one of the others was saying. Sometimes you just can't win. But what I go through is nothing in comparison to what the really big names put up with, and I have to say some handle it better than others. That was one of the things I really admired about Alfie. He was probably the most popular person in Queensland at his peak, and people were always coming up to him, day and night. I reckon he never changed. It was always 'G'day mate, how are ya?' The day a bloke like Alfie has to get a bodyguard is the day we all should seriously wonder if we'd be better off doing something else.

Of course all this sort of stuff was the furthest thing from my mind in 1993. All I had to worry about then was staying in the squad and doing the job Brian wanted me to do. Luckily it worked out better than I could have hoped. In the last match of the season Saints played the Broncos at ANZ Stadium. If we won we would finish minor premiers; if we lost, we'd finish fifth. There was a record crowd – over 58,000 – and Saints won 16–10. It was a huge result for the club. I was watching from the grandstand that day, even though I'd been playing first grade for a few weeks, replacing David Barnhill who was injured. He came back for the Broncos match and did his calf muscle, which meant I was back in for the semi-finals. Our first game was against Canberra. We won 31–10. The next week we beat Canterbury 27–10 and went straight into the Grand Final. I thought I was a chance to be in the run-on side for the game but David was passed fit and got his spot back, with me named on the bench. I suppose I was a little disappointed, but he was a good player and he'd been in the side for 20 matches so I was really just lucky to be there at all. Again we found ourselves up against Brisbane and again they were just too good.

Afterwards Wayne Bennett said that the Broncos were out on their feet. While we'd had a week off, they'd had to get there the hard way, and by the time they got to the match they were struggling. Could have fooled us. The win wasn't as comprehensive as the year before – they got up 14–6 – but they scored three tries to nil and we were never really in the hunt. I didn't really make much of a contribution. Jason Stevens broke his thumb in the first tackle of the game and I thought Brian might move Barnhill to the front row and put me on but he put Jeff Hardy on instead. Looking back, it was a pretty low game. All I can say about my involvement is that I was there; that was about it. Our preparation was good, our side was good, but Brisbane just had that extra bit of brilliance when they needed it.

WAYNE BENNETT: I never really noticed him when he was at St George. We didn't discuss him at our pre-game talks but we did a good job on him. I do remember Wendell put one of the best hits of his career on him. He played against us in the 1993 Grand Final, but to be honest, I didn't notice him. He told me he was there but he didn't make a big impact.

Brian did everything he could to help us win that Grand Final, but it just never clicked. There was one moment I'll never forget, though, and it happened the day before the game. We went out to the Sydney Football Stadium for our last training session and Brian had us all pumped up. When we got off the bus at the start of the long pathway leading to the entrance gates there was this groundsman driving around in a little golf cart. He stopped and offered us a ride. Mick Potter jumped in and off they went, up the path and back. As they headed down towards us Scottie Gourley yelled out, 'Hey, you'll need this' and threw a ball at them. Well the driver tried to be a smartarse and catch the ball one-handed, but he lost control of the cart and it smashed into one of the trees that lined the path. Mick Potter flew out of his seat, went straight over the front, did a somersault and landed flat on his back. Fair dinkum, we all fell on the ground we were laughing so hard. Brian was absolutely spitting chips. I'd never seen him so furious. Here he'd been getting us all ready for the biggest game of our lives, and because of some lunatic in a golf cart our star fullback is lying on his back half unconscious and the rest of us are rolling around giggling like lunatics. I don't think we ever recovered.

That made it two Grand Finals for two losses for Brian; another was to come in 2001 with Parramatta. I don't know why he can't get a team over the line. I still think he is a very good coach, especially for young blokes. Maybe that's his problem, he's too good. He doesn't leave anything to the players. He works out every move they should make and then, if things go wrong, they don't know what to do. There's no Plan B. I don't think that was the problem at Saints; I reckon we were just up against an outstanding side in the Broncos. No team could have beaten them. But with Parramatta in 2001 he probably had the best team in the competition. I knew it wouldn't be as cut and dried as everyone thought, though, which is why I tipped Newcastle that day. I thought that if Newcastle got off to a good start the Eels would struggle. You could tell that from playing both teams throughout the season. The Newcastle blokes would have a beer with you after the game, they were more like Brisbane, laid-back, enjoying themselves more. More a team. The Eels came across as arrogant, and I think that starts with the coach.

Not that I had too many problems with Brian at Saints. The media tried to make out that we were at loggerheads because he was playing me off the bench, but any fights we had weren't over that. They were over little things that just blew up. Our biggest clash when I was at Saints came in 1995, when we had a shocker versus Newcastle. Brian called an optional sprint session the next day and only six blokes turned up, which made him furious. I couldn't go because I was picking Mum up from the airport, and at training the next day he asked me where I had been. When I told him I was picking up my mother he said, 'Is your Mum going to do your tackling for you on the weekend?' I told him to get stuffed and we started getting into it. He said to me, 'Listen here, son', and I said, 'Don't call me "son"; you're not good enough to be my father', and so it went on. I didn't finish that session. Another time he got stuck into me for wearing a Super League cap to training in the middle of the controversy over whether Saints should stay with the ARL or not. He reckoned it was a stupid thing to do because he was trying to keep our minds on football. That was probably a fair gripe, so I copped that one on the chin.

The real bust-up between us happened in 2002, after the Broncos played Parramatta in a Friday night game. I was having my much-publicised problem with referees then, and after the game the Eels' centre, Michael Buettner, told the press that Brian had sent them out to gee-up the ref and try to get me sin-binned or sent off. The papers said Buettner told them that Smith gave them instructions to say to the ref, 'Hey ref, he can't say that about you' whenever I was near them. It sounds like school playground stuff now but back then it was serious. I was right in the middle of a really bad time in my career, with people calling for me to be sacked as Queensland and Broncos captain because of my problems with Bill Harrigan. The last thing I needed was for the selectors to be thinking I was a liability who could be targeted by opposition coaches. The Saturday morning after the story appeared, a

Brisbane reporter named Michael Westlake rang me and asked me what I thought. I said if Brian had done that then he wasn't the coach I thought he was. I said if that was the best he could come up with he was scraping the bottom of the barrel and must be struggling for ideas. Mike Westlake went back to Brian for his comments on what I had said and the next thing my mobile is ringing. Brian Smith calling. I was at the races with some of the boys by this time, and I'd had a few drinks, so I really went off at him. He said, 'Do you believe everything you read in the papers?' I said, 'I do when it's your own blokes who are saying it.' Then I hung up on him. Next he sent me a text message which said, 'I used to have respect for you but you've lost it as a player and a man.' I sent him one back that said 'I can't wait to play your team again, they're so soft.'

The Sunday Mail, 9 June 2002:
GORDIE GETS VERBALLED
by Michael Westlake

Gorden Tallis yesterday slammed Parramatta coach Brian Smith for trying to exploit the Brisbane captain's recent clashes with referees as a match tactic against the Broncos on Friday night.

A fuming Tallis described his former coach as 'two-faced' after Eels centre Michael Buettner admitted Smith had instructed Eels players – clearly audible through the referee's microphone – to pressure referee Tim Mander by complaining about Tallis's behaviour.

Eels captain Nathan Cayless accused an unidentified Broncos player of calling Mander 'a cheat' late in the game, an obvious reference to when Tallis was sent off for calling Bill Harrigan a cheat during an Origin clash in 2000, to try to get a reaction from Mander.

Buettner confessed after the game he was 'just following the coach's orders' to try to pressure the referee into penalising the Queensland captain.

Tallis said it was a 'dog act' for Smith – his coach at St George from 1992 to 1995 – to ride on the recent controversy about his dealings with referees to win the game.

'I thought we had a good relationship,' Tallis said. 'Every time I saw him, I'd like to speak to him. So it disappoints me he comes out with this. He tells his players to drag my name through the mud, then he has the hide to give me a friendly wave on his way to the press conference after the game.

'That's low and two-faced. Why would he do it? If he hates me that much, or wants to win games that much, then the bloke has got problems. Maybe he would be better served sending out instructions on how to score tries rather than how to milk the ref. Maybe he should coach players rather than referees. For him to exploit my personal situation for the benefit of his team is a low act. It is ridiculous if he wants to win a game of footy by having a cheap shot at me.'

Smith phoned Tallis yesterday after being contacted by The Sunday Mail, *and said their friendship was in place.*

It was all great stuff. Even Brownie got involved. He'd spoken to Brian, and rang me and told me I should pull back a bit, so I gave it to him too. I made it up with Brownie, but I haven't made it up with Brian and probably never will. At the World Sevens, before the 2003 season, I had to arrive early to do something for the new NRL TV commercial. I walked in to the stadium and it was empty except for me, Chris Walker who was on the oval warming up, and Brian, who was sitting in the stand. I walked past him and he turned the other way. Looks like it's still no-talkies. Pity, because we worked well together at one stage.

BRIAN SMITH: Gorden had got some very, very bad information which was disappointing to me, especially after I had gone to the trouble of contacting him. I found out later that he had had a few drinks when I rang and if I'd know that, I wouldn't have tried to contact him at that time. I feel sorry for him because there was no reason for any of that to happen. Gorden is always very loyal to the people who have helped him along the way and I hope we can get back to where we were. It's water off a duck's back to me but I understand how it happened. It's not the first time that someone has had their head filled with crap by someone else. It's happened to all of us at some stage.

But back to 1993. That year first grade headed to Hawaii for the end of season trip. This time I was eligible to go and it was the best time of my life – for all of two nights. The problem was that I was still 20, eight months off my 21st, and you have to be 21 to get into a bar in the US. For two nights I had no worries. I looked about 30 and the bouncers just let me straight in. We were having a ball, going into nightclubs and watching things like the Miss Hawaii bikini contest. Then there was a big crackdown, mainly because one of our guys, namely Nathan Brown, looked about 14. A couple of the blokes had taken their older brother's driver's licence with them, so they were fine. All I had to do was borrow Wally's licence, but I didn't think of it. So thanks to Brownie not looking old enough to shave, he and I spent the next six nights drinking beer in my hotel room. The good news was that you could buy Fourex at an ABC Store down the street, and we didn't have to suffer the hangovers the older blokes got.

And so ended my second year in Sydney. Already I'd done more than I'd ever thought possible: made first grade, got my picture in the paper, played in a Grand Final and built a garden bed, but the best was yet to come. And soon.

CHAPTER FOUR

HAIR TODAY, GONE TOMORROW

I found out I'd been picked for State of Origin from an old lady in a hairdressing salon in Hurstville. Not quite how you imagine it will happen, but like any rugby league player, I'll take news like that any way it comes.

It was the second game of the 1994 series, the one after the match where Mark Coyne scored that miracle try in the last seconds. What isn't remembered as fondly about that game is Martin Bella getting thumped in a tackle and getting up and playing the ball backwards. The selectors decided that Marty had had enough, so they dropped him and started looking around for a new option. What they came up with was me – thanks, I'm sure, to the fact that I was making an impact off the bench for St George. Darren Fritz went off the bench into Marty's front row spot and I took Darren's place on the bench, even though I took some convincing when I heard the news.

The funny thing was, when I made the Origin team the media was stirring up trouble about the way Brian was using me off the bench for St George. They reckoned I was being wasted, but I probably wouldn't have got the Origin call-up if I hadn't shown I could be effective off the bench. To be honest, I never had a problem with being a bench player back then. Any tension between me and Brian over the matter was pure paper-talk. As far as I was concerned, he was the coach, and if he thought that was the best way to use me, I was happy to go along with him. After all, it was working. I was coming into the game fresh and going crazy for 15 minutes at a time; I was still getting about 60 minutes a game and we were winning. Where was the problem? Plus, it got me that first Origin jersey.

As I said, I found out in a hairdressing joint at Hurstville. The wife of one of the players worked there, so whenever we needed a haircut, that's where we headed. This day I'd gone in there for a bit of a trim, and as I was waiting, this old lady getting a perm said to me: 'You're in the Origin team, eh?' I said to her, 'Not me, lady, I'm just a bench player for Saints.' 'No,' she said. 'You're Tallis, aren't you? I heard it on the radio, you're in the Origin team.' I wanted to run straight out of there and find out, but I was afraid of making an idiot of myself and losing my spot in line for a haircut. Plus I didn't believe it. Queensland selectors are known for their loyalty. They rarely make unforced changes, especially after they've just won a game. So I got my haircut, walked out of the shop – then sprinted to the nearest public phone and rang Mum.

I didn't get the chance to ask her if the news was right because as soon as she heard my voice she said: 'Where have you been? Everyone is after you. You're in the Origin team.' When I got back to my unit there were 40 messages on my answering machine, from Queensland boss Ross Livermore, all my mates from Townsville and everyone at St George. I was supposed to be in Queensland to go into camp that day but because of that haircut I couldn't get on a flight until the next day. It was probably a blessing. In those days, all it meant was that I missed out on a major drinking session.

When I arrived at the Brisbane Travelodge the first person I saw was the team's assistant manager, Choppy Close. I said hi to him and he just said, 'G'day mate' and kept walking. He didn't have a clue who I was. I had to run after him and say, 'I'm Gorden. Gorden Tallis? I'm in the side.' It wasn't the best start, but I soon found out nothing in Origin camp was the way I expected it to be.

CHRIS CLOSE: *He was just a young man when he walked into that hotel for the first time. He was very quiet, very shy, but I've seen a lot of young men in that situation and it's very easy to tell what their attitude is going to be. I looked at Gorden's eyes and they were on fire. He would have ripped the wallpaper off the walls and pulled the nails out of the foundations if those were the instructions. I could see how serious he was.*

He has changed a lot since then, of course; he's not the shy kid any more. He is a very confident, charismatic person. The thing about him is that he had a very good upbringing. His parents are wonderful people and they instilled confidence in him. He's had a great foundation in life. There's no anger in Gorden, no stupidity or sneakiness – he's straight down the line. He has self-confidence, and that allows him to be himself. He's got that incredible enthusiasm. He is high on life and it's infectious. Sometimes it just spills over. At training you'll hear Wayne Bennett call out, 'Gorden, go and take your tablet and calm down, will you?' He's a very strong person morally. He has certain beliefs about our game and he has the courage to tell people concerned exactly what he thinks.

As an Origin player, well, he is at the very top. When I think of outstanding moments in Origin, they revolve around aggression. There was Arthur Beetson in the very first game, when he tore into the opposition with no fear and total disregard for personal safety. There was 1981, when I backhanded Eric Grothe, and the time when Mal Meninga nearly killed Michael O'Connor in a tackle. Mate, that was dead-set scary. And there was Gorden Tallis in 2002 tackling that little fullback Hodgson and dragging him over the sideline like a rag doll. He could have just dominated him in the tackle but he did more than that. He totally demoralised him, and he demoralised the rest of the team too. That to me was a defining moment in Origin history. It is one of the things which will be remembered and played time and time again as an example of what Origin is all about. It is an example of what Gorden Tallis is all about as well.

Choppy took me up to the floor which had been taken over by the team. The guys were wandering around waiting to have their medicals and I was taking it all in like a kid in a lolly shop. There was this frosted glass wall and behind it I could see Mal Meninga's silhouette. I was totally overawed, but it was about to get worse. Around the corner walked our coach – Wally Lewis. These were the blokes whose pictures I'd had up on my bedroom wall in Townsville just two years earlier, and now I was supposed to be one of them. It seemed like it was all happening to someone else. Just then Tosser Turner, the team manager, walked down the hallway, followed by a Channel 9 camera crew. They were doing a special feature on Tosser and following him around for the day. He walked down the hall saying hello to all the press who were standing there and asking everyone if everything was okay, looking like he was totally in control. Then he went to go into his room and he couldn't get the door open. He was pushing and shoving, and his face was going redder and redder, and the cameraman was filming it all. Finally Tosser put his shoulder against the door and pushed it open, and these two little faces poked out, laughing like schoolkids. That was my introduction to Alfie Langer and Kevvie Walters, the Brownie and Goldie of Queensland. The next day we went to Villanova College pool for a swimming session. Brian Canavan was the trainer and he was standing there in his bright new Queensland shirt and shorts and running shoes with his clipboard, telling us what he wanted us to do, when Mal Meninga walked over, picked him up and threw him into the pool. I remember thinking 'Holy ghost, this would never happen at St George.'

That's how it was the whole camp. Alfie was so funny, he

started me laughing that week and I never stopped for the next ten years. I must admit, though, that it took me a little bit of time to work him out. These days I'm probably the biggest pest in camp, going around and geeing people up, but back then I didn't say a word. I was this shy kid trying to work out what was going on. Alfie and Kevvie were so close; they'd grown up together in Ipswich and they were like a comedy act which had been on the road for years. They had little routines, and if you hadn't been around for a while you could get pretty confused. Like their fake fist fights. They'd been doing that since they were kids, and gee it looked real. They'd pretend to pick a fight over something and the next thing they'd be throwing punches and rolling around, and people walking past would think they were killing each other. There was another thing they used to do when we were driving through town in the team bus. Whenever Alfie saw a, shall we say, large and rather unattractive woman he'd call out, 'Hey Kim, Kim.' Kim was the name of Kev's wife, and Alf would say, 'Geez Kevvie, Kim's let herself go a bit. Why do you let her eat so much?' And Kev would be like, 'Don't you talk about her like that, it's only a couple of pounds' and the next thing they'd be rolling around in the aisle of the bus pretending to kill each other again. Blokes like Big Mal would be cacking themselves laughing because they knew what was going on, but I'd be thinking, 'Gee, Alfie's being pretty rude about Kev's wife.' I didn't know which way to look because I was so embarrassed. The first time I saw the real Kim I couldn't believe how attractive she was. I guess I was pretty naive, but if you weren't used to Alfie and Kevvie you could get left behind big-time.

Right through camp Alfie was always coming out with

these little one-liners and geeing everyone up – from Wally down. That's how it is with Alfie. He isn't impressed by reputation or titles. The bigger someone gets, the more likely Alfie is to have a crack at them. I think that's why he worked so well with Wayne Bennett. If you don't know him, Wayne can come across as a pretty cold character, but he's really not like that. He likes a laugh and he loves it when Alfie has a shot at him. One of the things that made the Broncos so successful over the years is the way Alfie kept everyone's feet on the ground. If he thought someone was getting a bit ahead of themselves he'd bring them back down to earth pretty quick.

That Origin campaign was the first time I really had a chance to talk to Wayne. I remember talking to him at an after-match function. I said to him, 'How do you coach these blokes?', and before he had a chance to answer, Alfie bobbed up and said: 'What are you talking about? I coach the team, he just looks good.' Wayne just laughed. He loved it. I couldn't help thinking how much fun all the Broncos players seemed to be having. It wasn't that I wasn't having fun at St George, but this was different. They were all such close mates and so laid-back. Football didn't seem to be the life and death situation it was in Sydney.

When I joined the club a few years later, I learnt that that was a bit of an illusion. No team trains harder than the Broncos, no-one wants to win more and no-one is under such pressure to win. Sometimes you feel that while other clubs' supporters want them to win, the Broncos supporters expect them to win. From the outside, looking in, it seemed effortless. I can tell you it isn't. Whenever a player joins the Broncos from another club, they comment on how hard we train and how competitive the players are. The reason it looks so much fun is because it is. The players are very tight with each other because we live so close. Playing in Sydney, you might have players living across three or four suburbs. Some drive for close to an hour to get to training, and when they head off after a game you don't see them again until the next training session. At the Broncos nearly everyone lives a few minutes from each other, and whenever something is on, like a golf day or a trip to the races, everyone is there. The closest a Sydney club has to that is Cronulla. They all live in what they call 'The Shire' and stick together, and of course the one-town one-club places like Newcastle, Canberra and Auckland have the same thing. But for me back in 1994 it was all new. I had come from St George to Origin camp and walked straight into this environment where the majority of the players were from the Broncos. They were such close mates and having so much fun together that it just blew me away. It seemed as if they weren't under as much pressure as players from Sydney and with two premierships on the trot everything looked to be going as smooth as silk.

Unfortunately, the same couldn't be said about that Origin campaign. I played my first game at the Melbourne Cricket Ground and didn't do anything wrong, but we lost 14–nil in front of nearly 90,000 people – only the second time Queensland had ever failed to score a point in an Origin game. I have to say I wasn't too devastated by the result. I was just so happy to be part of the team that the game was almost secondary. It was such an incredible experience for me, just like it is for everyone who realises a dream and plays Origin, that memories of the game itself aren't the main part. To tell you the truth, I didn't even watch much of it as I sat on the bench. I was too busy looking down at my jersey. I couldn't believe I was wearing it and couldn't stop staring at it. That's probably how I first hurt my neck. It was all amazing, from the time I got the news at that hairdressing salon to the minute we broke up and headed home after the match, but I suppose it could have been even better. When you are a kid growing up in Queensland you dream about running on for your first Origin match at Lang Park and walking off a winner. Playing in Melbourne and losing wasn't quite what I had imagined. When you look at all those young Queenslanders who debuted in that incredible win at Lang Park in 2001, you can see that the memories of their first Origin will be better than mine, but I certainly wasn't complaining at the time.

Now that I'm a bit older and more experienced, I can see that there was a bit of a problem in that team. I would never bag Wally Lewis, he was the best player of all time in my book, but he was really up against it that year. Coaching blokes you played with is never easy, and coaching blokes like Alfie and Kevvie in Origin must be almost impossible. A rep coach is different from a club coach. He has about five days to get the blokes together, working as a team and thinking the same way. How much can you teach a player in five days? Not much. All you can do is go out for a beer, try to pass on a couple of moves and build up some spirit. That's why Chris Anderson has been so successful as Australian coach. He's one of the blokes – when the time is right he gets serious, but somehow he also manages to get 17 blokes who have tried to bash each other's brains out in club and Origin football to work together as a team when they put on that green and gold jersey. Wally tried to do the same thing, but having been a player himself just a year or two earlier, it was tough.

Another thing which made the job harder for Wally was that Origin was starting to go through a bit of a transition. In the early days, when Artie Beetson was coach, Origin was like a big party. The players would go out on the grog for three nights in a row, do a little bit of training, go out for lunch, have a water-pistol fight, go out on the grog again and then play the game. By the time I got into the side things were starting to change. It was still great fun, but there was a serious element as well. These days we go into camp at a place in the Gold Coast hinterland that you practically can't get to unless you have a four-wheel drive. There is no nightclub within 20 km, and when we aren't training or talking about the game we are playing Pictionary or euchre. It wasn't anything like that back in 1994; it was starting to change, though, and unfortunately for Wally, he was the man in the middle.

I didn't realise it at the time because I was hanging off every word Wally said, but I think there was a little bit of tension there. During his playing days Wally enjoyed camp as much as anyone, but as a coach there were a couple of times when he told the boys to tone it down a bit or lay off the beers. A couple of them would be like, 'You're kiddin', Wally – when you were playing you were one of the worst', and when Wally told us not to have a drink, Alfie would walk out the door saying, 'Yeah, no worries, Wally, just six beers and a headlock.' I see it myself today, now that Glenn Lazarus and Kevvie are assistant coaches at the Broncos. If they try to tell me something I can't help saying, 'Yeah, right' and making a joke, but I see the younger blokes taking it all on board. That's not to say Wally wasn't a good coach; I reckon he was. He was just as well prepared and organised as any coach I've ever had, and if you put him in charge of

Origin today it would be a totally different story, but back then he was up against it, especially because he was such a huge figure in the game. When we arrived in Melbourne he was the only one anyone wanted to talk to; he was the focus of all the stories and that just added to the pressure. Plus Wally had been so successful on the field for Queensland. If the team needed something miraculous to pull them out of trouble, he'd do it. Sitting on the sidelines seeing things unfold on the field and not being in a position to take control himself must have been very frustrating for him.

We had a good time, though. Wally was still the bus driver, as he had been in his playing days, and Alfie was always geeing him up to do something. He'd be, 'Hey Wally, I bet you fifty cents you can't drive up on the curb' or 'Wally, I bet you 50 cents you can't get in front of this bloke in the ute.' It was always 50 cents. Wally took it all. The one thing he didn't like was being called 'The King'. One time we were all piling into the bus in our tracksuits after training and these Japanese tourists started taking photos of us. Alfie yelled out, 'Hey Wally, they recognise you. Listen, I can hear them calling out "Long Ling Le Ling, Long Ling Le Ling".' Wally drove back to the hotel fuming with Alfie chanting 'Long Ling Le Ling' all the way.

With the series locked up at one–all, the decider being at Lang Park and it being Big Mal's last game for Queensland, I was obviously dead keen to make the side, so when Wally pulled me aside after the Melbourne game and said he wanted me to have a big one for St George on the weekend, I took the tip: if I wanted another Origin jersey I had to show a bit of mongrel. Unfortunately, I took him a bit too literally, and managed to get sent off for headbutting.

We were playing Newcastle at Marathon, which is always enough to get me pretty fired up anyway, and when Jamie Ainscough elbowed me in the face as we lay on the ground after I'd tackled him, I lashed out with my head. Greg McCallum took one look and pointed to the sheds. I was sent off for the first time in my life. The Queensland selectors did the right thing by me and named me subject to the judiciary's decision, but you'd have to say I was at long odds to get off. I'll say one thing: if I'd been playing for the Broncos back then I wouldn't have been a hope, but with Geoff Carr in my corner I had a slim chance. Geoff was manager of the NSW side back then and the Blues and Maroons both went into camp on the day of the judiciary hearing. For the second game in a row I missed day one. That night Geoff took me along to the hearing and he was absolutely brilliant. One thing in my favour was the fact that I'd missed Ainscough's head and hit him on the neck; the other was this cock and bull story that Geoff dreamed up in my defence. He told the judiciary that as part of our training at St George we'd had this wrestling coach teach us wrestling moves. Geoff reckoned that thanks to my wrestling training I had actually been pulling my head out of the way in self-defence to avoid further attacks from Ainscough. By the end of it he almost had me believing it. Also, it couldn't have hurt our case that on the video, when Ainscough got up he was holding the side of his face – but it was the other side, not the one I'd hit. Anyway, I got off and Geoff invited me out for a drink to celebrate.

He was staying at the Coogee Bay Travelodge with the NSW team but he reckoned they were all out at a sponsor's promotion, so even though the last thing I wanted to do was bump into any of the NSW players, we went there. I was sitting in the bar having a beer or two with Geoff, when in walked Brad Mackay and Dave Barnhill, two of my teammates from Saints who were in the NSW side. We had a couple more with them and then a few more of the Blues drifted in. And a few more and a few more. Soon there we all were, me and the NSW Blues drinking and joking and everyone was saying how lucky I was to get off – especially Chris Johns, who was with the Broncos. I won't say by the end of the night we all had our arms around each other singing the NSW team song, but it was close. I staggered out of there about 1 am feeling no pain. I don't know if it was a NSW tactic, but it worked. The next morning I was as crook as a dog.

I would have missed my 9 am plane to Brisbane if my flatmate, Luke Felsch, hadn't woken me up. By the time I arrived at the Brisbane Travelodge I hadn't improved much. Wally took one look at me and said, 'What happened to you?' I told him I ate something bad on the plane and headed for my room. I was lying on my bed and Steve Walters came in straight from his medical, dressed in nothing but his jocks. He went up to the mirror and started doing all these muscle flexes like he was in the Mr Universe contest, then turned to me and said, 'So tell me, what's it like rooming with the best player in the world?' It was good to be back.

Unfortunately, Mal's last Origin game didn't turn out to be the fairytale ending we'd all hoped for. It was a disaster from the kick-off. Jason Smith had come into the side as play-maker and a lot of our work during the week had revolved around him. Early in the match we were attacking and the Blues came off their line in defence. Ian Roberts charged at Jason Smith, who didn't have the ball, and cleaned him up on suspicion. They smashed heads and Jason was out like a light with a broken cheekbone. He was carried off on a stretcher as his brother Darren went on to replace him. It wasn't the best start and it didn't get a whole lot better, for me or the team. Right before half-time I made a break and landed on my elbow as I tried to palm off Ricky Stuart. Andrew Gee scored a couple of plays later, but by then I was in too much pain to notice. At half-time the doctor told me my elbow was dislocated. He strapped it up in the hope that I'd be able to go back on but it cooled down in the break and I couldn't move it. That was it for me, and for Wally, too. With me, Willie Carne and Jason Smith all injured, we went down 27–12, losing the series. Wally's coaching career was over.

I went back to Sydney with my elbow all strapped up, thinking I would be out for a few weeks. As it was I only missed two games – but the second one was a good one not to be involved in. Saints went to Brookvale to play Manly and got caught by Cliff Lyons on one of his 'on' days, probably the on-est day he'd ever had. Manly scored 12 tries and won 61–nil, the worst loss in St George's history. I played the next week when we turned things around against Wests, but our season was all but finished. Mine certainly was. In Round 19 we had a Saturday night match against Balmain. I tore the ligaments in my ankle and that was it for 1994.

I didn't need an operation but I was on crutches and couldn't walk for six weeks. Still, I was reasonably happy with my season. I'd played Origin and cemented a spot in first grade. And I'd also started to make some real money. Soon after I arrived in Sydney I met a great mate of Brad Mackay's named Darryl Mather, who was a keen rugby league supporter. Darryl was a good bloke who worked in an executive role for the clothing group Country Road, and he knew some of the St George players such as Brownie. Darryl would come to all the games and we used to go around to his house to eat pizza and watch the Friday night games on TV. It was a lot more comfortable than our place, I can tell you. Darryl and I got to be mates, and late in the 1994 he asked me how the club was treating me. I told him I had no complaints. After all, I was earning $9000 a year and together with the money I was making working for the council I thought I was doing pretty well. He nearly fell off his chair. 'Nine thousand bucks? Mate, you're an Origin player, they're robbing you.' He said I should march into Geoff Carr's office and demand more money, but that wasn't my way. I was just happy to be playing the game. Darryl asked me if I'd like him to have a word to them and I said sure. When he came back to me it was my time to fall off the chair. He got me over $100,000 a year for two years plus a big whack for the season so far.

From then on Darryl looked after me, just as a mate, but before the end of the year he told me it was getting a bit much for him. He had a top-level job and was just helping me out as a favour, and I was getting offers for things like boot and gear sponsorships. I couldn't believe it. When I'd come to Sydney I could hardly afford to buy a decent pair of boots. Now people were offering me money to wear theirs. It wasn't Darryl's go, so he put me together with a friend of his named George Mimis. George was a top operator, a former merchant banker who represented some of the biggest names in the game. He had Brad Clyde, who was probably the best forward in the world then, and up and comers like Jack Elsegood and Brownie. You could say he specialised in good-looking players, but he took me on anyway.

With George looking after me, Saints doing the right thing and a couple of Origin jerseys in the wardrobe the future looked bright, not just for me, but also for the game. With four new teams coming in and public interest in rugby league sky-high we all thought 1995 was going to be a big year. We didn't know the half of it.

CHAPTER FIVE

APRIL FOOLS

It was 6.30 am, April Fool's Day 1995, the day before a game, and the phone was ringing. Nobody woke me up early before a game – not my family, not my friends. I staggered to the phone, thinking, 'This had better be important.' It was.

George Mimis was on the phone, and after apologising for waking me up, he told me what everyone with an interest in rugby league was about to find out. The rumours about News Limited planning to take over the game and form a Super League weren't rumours any more. It had happened.

As I said earlier, George managed Brad Clyde, who was

one of the biggest names in the game and about to come off contract. News Limited had an interest in Brad's club Canberra, and when James Packer had made a huge offer to get Brad across to his favourite club, Easts, Canberra chief executive Kevin Neil rang News Limited boss Ken Cowley asking for help. Ken told him to sit tight because the cavalry was on its way. From what I'm told it was Easts' bid for Clyde which pushed Super League forward again after Kerry Packer had knocked it on the head by threatening to sue any club which tried to break away. News Limited went to their lawyers, who said Packer couldn't win. Then it was on for young and old. George got the tip-off on the morning of Friday 31 March, when a News Limited executive rang and told him to get on the afternoon flight to Townsville. Canberra were playing the Cowboys the next night and before the game News Limited signed them all up. They wanted George there to make sure that Clyde signed on the spot. The next morning, bright and early, George was on the phone to me.

'Gordie,' he said. 'Super League is here. This player and that player have signed and these clubs have gone over . . .' He was naming blokes like Brad Clyde, Laurie Daley and Terry Lamb, and clubs like Canberra, Canterbury and the Cowboys, and saying how Newcastle and the Broncos were expected to go over and I was like, 'What the hell's going on?' He told me he was booked on the first flight back from Townsville on Sunday and he'd be coming straight to Kogarah, where we were playing Canterbury. And not to do anything until he got there. I went back to bed with my head spinning. I'd gone to sleep with everything being a certain way and when I woke up my whole world was turned upside down.

Sure enough, Geoff Carr tried to get us all to sign an ARL

loyalty agreement before the game. He didn't say we couldn't play if we didn't sign, but it was still pretty heavy. The team used to get together before a home game. Geoff wasn't usually there, but he turned up this day and he and Brian Smith got up and told us that this organisation – News Limited – was trying to buy the game. They said it was a two-dollar shelf company and the takeover had no merit and couldn't possibly work. Then Geoff put all these contracts on a table and said, 'Now if you'll sign this I'll give you a $20,000 loyalty payment.' There was no talk of, 'If you don't sign you won't be able to play today', but you could tell Geoff would have loved us to sign. Some blokes jumped in but I'd been clued up by George so I just said, 'I ain't signing anything. I've got a manager' and headed off to play footy.

After the game, George arrived and came back to the club with us. The team used to go into a special room and have a meal so George came in and sat down with me and Brownie. He told us just to sit tight and see what was on offer before we jumped at anything. Geoff Carr came over every now and then and upped the ante on the loyalty agreement. It was a pretty interesting meal. By the time we got dessert that $20,000 had grown to $100,000.

On Tuesday morning, along with just about everyone else in the game, I went down to ARL headquarters in Phillip Street to see what was happening. It was like nothing you could ever imagine. There were dozens of players down there lining the corridors, sitting on seats if they could find them or on the floor if they couldn't, waiting to get into a room so James Packer, Bob Fulton or Phil Gould could hand them a pile of money. Brownie and I got there at 9 am and we weren't the first, that's for sure. It was the same day that

Paul Harragon drove a bus down from Newcastle with all the Knights senior players. Add them to the blokes who were already there, and it was some crowd. I sat there from 9 am to at least 4 pm, talking to other players, such as Brett Dallas, and waiting to get in and get my cut.

George knew there was going to be a big wait so he told me to give him a call on his mobile when I was getting close. His office was only a few minutes away, so when I finally got in to see Phil Gould, George was there with me. Thinking back on it now, it might have been better if I'd gone in by myself, because it was pretty obvious that the ARL was dirty on George. Because he had gone up to Townsville – the only manager to get the chance to be with his client on that first weekend – the ARL saw him as a Super League man. It was a pretty weird time. They called it the Super League war, and it was like war. People who had known each other for a long time were suddenly on different sides and it became pretty personal, especially in the ARL bunker where 'Bozo' Fulton and 'Gus' Gould were in charge of signing up players. They were both pretty competitive guys who had played footy, and getting stuck into Super League was like playing the game again. They really threw themselves into it. So when I walked in with George beside me Gus wasn't exactly rolling out the red carpet.

The thing was, as far as I was concerned, George was always just there to advise me and handle negotiations. The final decision was always going to be up to me, and when I arrived at the ARL that morning I fully intended to sign for them. I was very happy at St George, all my mates were signing up with the ARL and I certainly didn't want to go off on my own. If they'd done the right thing by me I would have had no problems staying put, but that's not what happened.

When the ARL got organised, it had worked out a set level of payments for their loyalty agreements. A first grader got $50,000, a fringe representative $100,000, a State of Origin player $150,000 and an Australian representative $200,000. That was the minimum. It was negotiable, and some of the top Australian players got a lot more. It really depended on how much they wanted you and how big a tactical move it was in terms of keeping your club loyal. According to the figures that came out in the court case, Paul Harragon got $650,000 and Mark Coyne, as Saints were wavering about going to Super League, got $543,000. Andrew and Matthew Johns got over $500,000 each and neither of them had played Origin at that stage.

I wasn't after any more than what I thought I was entitled to. I'd played State of Origin so I thought I should get $150,000, just like every other Origin player. It didn't take long to realise that Gus had other ideas.

'He's just a bench player,' he said to George. 'He can't even get off the bench for his club. Why should we give him Origin money?'

When you put it that way, he was probably right. I was a bench player at Origin level and Brian Smith did use me off the bench at Saints, but that's how he thought I was of best use for the team. I'd had plenty of offers from other clubs, such as Balmain and Souths, who had told me they wouldn't be using me off the bench, but I was happy to stay with Saints. Plus I was 20 years old. You don't have to be Einstein to work out that someone who is in the Origin side at 20 probably has a reasonable future in the game, but Gould wasn't budging. He virtually told me he didn't rate me and that I should take what he was offering or hit the road. We hit the road.

The ARL's offer didn't push me to Super League – I would have listened to what they had to say anyway – but it sure didn't help. A couple of days after leaving Phillip Street, we went to Super League headquarters in an office building over the road from News Limited at Surry Hills. To say things were different over there would be selling it short. We sat in a waiting room on leather lounge chairs. There was a big Coke fridge full of soft drinks and juices, and a table of sandwiches and snacks.

George and I were seen by John Ribot and David Gallop. They told us all about the concept, how it would work and what the benefits would be for the players. They never even mentioned money the whole time. The thing that really made me sit up was when they said that I could pick the team I wanted to play for. My only question was: 'Can I play for the Broncos?'

After my experience with the Origin team that was the one thing that interested me. The thought of playing alongside Alfie Langer and Kevvie Walters was very attractive. Plus I knew I couldn't play for another club in Sydney. It was St George or nothing. I just couldn't imagine living in Sydney and not being with my mates from Saints. When I asked the question, they didn't say no. It was like well, we'll see what the roster is like, see whether they have taken up their quota and whether they have room on their books. It was all gibberish to me. I didn't know anything about quotas and rosters. All I knew was that if I was going to play for Super League it was going to be with the Broncos, end of story.

The next day they came back to George with an offer. It was good money, but I still wanted to know about playing for the Broncos. Over the next months they came back to me with every club but the Broncos – Adelaide, Perth, Penrith, Cronulla, Canterbury. I told George to tell them that if they thought I was leaving St George to go to Adelaide or Perth, they should think again. I now know that I was putting them under a lot of pressure. Here they were, trying to convince all the other clubs that this wasn't a competition set up by the Broncos, for the Broncos, and here I was, an Origin player, saying I wouldn't go anywhere else. It threatened the whole concept, because they really wanted a strong, even competition but I wasn't all that interested in that. They tried to make it more attractive by offering more money but I wouldn't budge. Finally John Ribot rang Broncos chief executive Shane Edwards, and Shane went down to training to see Wayne Bennett. Shane said, 'Gorden Tallis reckons he won't come over unless he plays for the Broncos' and Wayne said, 'Well, if he wants to come that much I suppose we'll have to take him.'

WAYNE BENNETT: When he came to us I'd have to say everyone else was more pumped up about it than I was. They told me he'd signed with Super League and he refused to go to the Cowboys; the only club he'd play with was the Broncos. Everyone was all excited, running around like chooks with their heads cut off, but I still hadn't seen him do much. Obviously, if he was coming I'd deal with it. He was keen and that pleased me. It didn't take long to like the bloke, because that's the sort of bloke he is. He's open as a book, but I still didn't know what I'd got my hands on. I know he'd had good games, but I just hadn't seen them. It was Blocker

Roach who first told me what we had. He came up to me and said, 'Wayne, I see you've got Gorden Tallis coming to the Broncos. Mate, he'll be sensational for you. He's my type of man.' I said, 'Is that so Blocker? Why's that?' He told me that he'd been at a disco on the Gold Coast where Gorden was and Sean Garlick, from the Roosters, had put shit on Gorden's sister. He didn't know it was Gorden's sister, but Gorden just went whack and knocked him out with one punch. Then he turned to Blocker and said, 'You can't let 'em put shit on your family, Block.' Garlick woke up and went over to about half a dozen of his mates and had a pow-wow. They wanted to fight Gorden. Gorden said, 'Look, I won't fight the six of you all at once but I'll fight you one at a time if that's what you want.' They just turned and walked off. I was told that story long before I knew him, but it told me he was a person with a lot of character. That's him: he says things and he does things full on.

Before I signed I'd got a call from Fatty Vautin. Wayne had been appointed to take over as Origin coach from Wally, but when he was told he couldn't pick Super League players he resigned and Fatty was appointed. As I still hadn't made up my mind and signed with either side, Fatty rang me and asked if I wanted to play Origin. Was he kidding? Of course I wanted to play. He was like, 'You beauty, you're in . . . as long as you sign an ARL loyalty agreement first.' I felt for Fatty, because NSW had all the big-name players and he was trying to get the best side that he could, but his hands were tied. Even though at that stage I was still an ARL player and hadn't signed anything with Super League, the heavies at the

ARL wouldn't let me play. For some reason they let Gavin Allen play, even though he was in the same situation. Obviously they needed front-rowers more than they needed back-rowers. It was pretty hard sitting at home and watching Origin on TV, but seeing Fatty's side wipe the Blues 3–nil made it a lot easier to take.

When George got the word back from Super League that I could go to the Broncos, I went to see Geoff Carr to give him the last option. When I told him what they had offered he said, 'Mate, we can't afford you, but listen, this Super League thing is a two-dollar shelf company. They'll never pay you.'

I said thanks and nodded my head as if I didn't have a worry in the world and got straight on the phone. 'George,' I said. 'It's a two-dollar shelf company. They'll never pay me.'

George said to relax. 'I guarantee you'll get paid,' he said. So I went back to Geoff for the last time. I told him I'd definitely be going unless he could give me a good reason to stay. Again he said Saints couldn't afford me, and then he added, 'But I'll give you a release at the end of the season.'

I can still hear him saying those words as if he was standing right in front of me now. With that undertaking, I went back to Super League and signed.

GEOFF CARR: We were never going to give him a release from his contract. It wouldn't have made any sense. He was contracted, simple as that. We were very keen to keep him, but we had very little money. We had a lot of young blokes we had brought through, and they were all coming off contract around the same time. They'd all made a name for themselves and had managers who were asking for big money. In a way we were victims of our own success. I can't remember the exact words, but when Gorden told me what the Broncos were offering I may have indicated that we would have difficulty matching it. He might have misconstrued that, but there was no way I meant we'd let him off the last year of his contract. We had a terrific group of players, and if we'd kept them together we could have done anything.

It was a relief to finally have it all sorted out and I threw myself into the season. There weren't too many problems in the club about my having signed with Super League because there were so many of us who had done it: Goldie, Brownie, Jason Stevens, Choc and I were all signed and headed to other clubs. On one occasion one of the ARL-signed players did his block during a game and told us that we should get off because 'you Super League blokes won't have a go', but it was sorted out pretty quickly and for the most part Saints just forgot about it and concentrated on doing well in 1995. There was even a lot of talk that Saints were going to go over to Super League, but that was before they held a big rally at the club and Johnny Raper and Graham Richardson told the members to vote against it. When Mark Coyne, who had signed an ARL loyalty agreement, came out onto the stage and announced that he'd just re-signed for Saints for three years on the proviso that they didn't go to Super League it swung the crowd the ARL's way. Even though the members were pro-ARL, the majority of players wanted Saints to play in Super League. We had a meeting one night at the club, just between ourselves, down where the Chinese restaurant used to be. There were 55 players there and when it came to the vote, 50 were for Super League. I know Super League really thought they had the club signed up, but in the end the board members pulled out because they were worried that if the competition fell over they could be held financially liable.

I don't know what I would have done if Saints had gone to Super League, but I do know it would have put me under a fair bit of pressure to stay put. Especially if the other Super League players – Brownie, Goldie, Choc and Jason – had stayed as well. I really liked the club and was really close to the other blokes. I had made a home there, but the truth is I was running out of patience with Sydney. The traffic was shocking, the cost of living was high and I missed the laid-back life of Queensland. On the up side, I had great memories of playing with my mates at Saints. But like I said, it was a strange time, and the club was going through upheaval. The battle was turning everything upside down and Geoff Carr reckoned Saints would fold if they didn't merge with Easts. That didn't exactly go over well with the St George support-ers. They held a rally where a couple of blokes carried in a coffin and Geoff got death threats. He had to have a police escort when he arrived at the ground for games. Soon after that he left and moved to ARL headquarters, and Brian John-ston took over. It was too late for Brian Smith; he'd already flown the coop. When the Saints–Easts merger looked like going ahead he saw the writing on the wall. Phil Gould, the

Roosters coach, was handling negotiations for Easts and it was pretty obvious that he would be the coach of the merged club. Brian quit and headed back to England to coach Bradford. Needless to say, all this didn't have me throwing high-fives. The last time I'd met Phil Gould he'd pretty well told me he didn't think I could play. As it turned out, with the members threatening to pull the club down brick by brick if they merged with Easts, the board voted to go it alone and there was no longer any question of Gus coaching a combined side. The board appointed Rod Reddy, but then he signed with Super League, so they brought in David Waite.

Somehow, through all this we managed to make the top eight. After being 17th after Round 6 we got on a bit of a roll and won nine of our last ten games. I can't speak for anyone else, but I know I was trying my guts out all season because I knew I wouldn't be around in 1996 and I wanted to go out on a high. As a matter of fact, it was easily my best season for the club; when I think about it, this could have been the reason Saints didn't want to let me go. Even though I had played Origin the year before, I was still looked at as a bench player by some people. In 1995 I had started to stand out. I got my first big rap in the *Rugby League Yearbook*. David Middleton, who writes it, said I 'emerged as one of the most damaging running forwards in years and carved up the opposition almost single-handedly on occasion'. I wonder if Phil Gould got a copy.

My best games were against Cronulla, where I only played about 30 minutes, and Auckland.

Daily Telegraph Mirror, 7 August 1995:
TALLIS THE MAN – MAGIC DRAGON ON REF'S REPORT AFTER CUTTING WOEFUL WARRIORS DOWN TO SIZE
By Lee Umbres

St George second-rower Gorden Tallis spearheaded his side to a 47–14 drubbing of Auckland at Ericsson Stadium yesterday, but the talented Tongan was lucky to stay on the field after uplifting Warrior Andy Platt in the fourth minute.

TV replays had the partisan Auckland crowd baying for Tallis's blood, but the big forward responded with a man-of-the-match performance, shredding the Warriors' defence almost at will.

St George coach Brian Smith said perhaps the trademark Auckland Polynesian drums would have 'stirred a bit of Gorden's (Tongan) blood'.

There were no weak links in his arsenal yesterday as he out-muscled the Warriors pack. Every time he ran with the ball he was able to dazzle the defence. As well as power, he showed incredible pace, sprinting past flying Auckland winger Sean Hoppe in an 80-metre dash to the posts.

Smith said Tallis was 'a young player with rough patches – but he's an awesome sight with ball in hand, isn't he?'

Tallis, 22, previously regarded as the Winfield Cup's super-sub, was given his chance in the starting line-up when star Saints second-rower Scott Gourley was sidelined for 12 weeks with injury.

'Hopefully I can stay off the bench,' Tallis said.

Tallis said he had been given 'a bit of a ribbing' by Smith at half-time after missing two tackles which led to tries. He responded immediately with the 80-metre dash 35 seconds into the second half.

When Tallis was rested on the bench for a spell in the second half the Auckland fans breathed a sigh of relief, but he returned after 10 minutes on the sidelines to lay on a try for centre Mark Bell.

The game I was happiest with was the semi-final against Canterbury.

It was some game, and I'm glad that it was the last one I got to play for Saints – I feel I really tried hard for the club right to the end. Actually, it was as if I had two farewell games. The first was our last home game at Kogarah. I remember that with about four games to go, Brian Smith came up to me and told me that he was leaving the club. He said I might only have four more games for Saints and that I should try to go out on top. I really took in what he said. Saints had been good to me, given me an opportunity when no-one else would, so I owed them. As a matter of fact, if I have just one regret in my entire career, it was that I never told Rod Reddy that I was leaving. He was the one who had brought me down and helped me get my chance, and when I left the club it looked as if he was going to be coach. I've always felt bad about the fact that I didn't go to see him and tell him that I was going and why.

That last game at Kogarah was against the Western Reds, and I remember being pretty sad as I was getting changed before kick-off. I knew we'd made the semis, and when you are in the play-offs you always run on thinking you've got another game next week, but this was different. No matter what happened in the finals, this was my last chance to play at Kogarah in front of the home crowd. Kogarah is a pretty small ground – it only holds about 15,000 – but boy they could make some noise. They were great supporters, very passionate, and you could tell that other clubs hated playing us there. I gave it everything, and when I walked off I knew I was leaving part of myself behind.

The next week was the elimination quarter-final against Canterbury. If ever there was a game that had everything, this was it. It was raining, and everyone was sliding around in the mud, but that didn't stop both teams really turning it on. We probably would have won if Choc had scored a try after about three minutes. Brownie put through a grubber and Choc chased it through. With the ground so wet he just had to dive on it to slide over the line, but then he tried to pick it up and knocked on. Then just before half-time he put us in front when he outpaced Brett Dallas, one of the fastest players in the game, to score a try. That was Choc for you. Gee, it was a good game. Everyone was giving it everything. Dean Pay and Simon Gillies carved us up and Brownie and Choc were giving them heaps around the ruck. There was a huge blue – one of the biggest I've ever seen. It started when Brownie was giving cheek in a scrum. With Stevens, Barnhill and Gourley to protect him, Brownie thought he was pretty safe, but Robert Relf reached through and belted him. As we were jogging away from the scrum I said to Relf, 'Mate, pick on someone your own size.' He came back and said, 'Do you want a go?' Or at least that's what he tried to say. He was about halfway through when I swung around and hit him with the best right hand I've ever thrown. From there it was on for young and old. It spilled right across the field to the sideline. I was trying to belt Relf again and Darren Britt got me in the choke hold. I got out of that, but then Dean Pay came in and king hit me on the side of the head. Geez, it hurt. I got sin-binned and so did Pay. The turning point came late, when Mark Coyne got obstructed by John Timu and Terry Lamb scored. We were screaming that it should be a penalty and Brian was going off his brain on the sideline but what can you do? They won 12–8 and went on to win the premiership. I don't know if we would have gone all the way, but we sure could have won that day, and if you look at the results from then on, no-one came close to them. Whenever I see their coach Chris Anderson I remind him how lucky the Bulldogs were that day.

CHRIS ANDERSON: He's always telling me how he bashed us that day and how lucky we were to get away with it. I'll say this for him: he was the only one from Saints who held his hands up. The one doing all the bashing that day was Dean Pay. He was giving it to them and Gordie gave some back. He really had a go, but as far as us being lucky, I don't think so. I know it was a really good tough game and we won it. I can appreciate that Gordie would say that, though. That's him, isn't it?

For me, walking off that day was one of those bitter-sweet experiences. I was happy in myself because I knew I'd played well and given it everything, but I was sad because I knew I wouldn't be playing with my mates from Saints again. After a game like that you usually go around the dressing room and shake hands with your team-mates, saying well done for the game and the season. This time when I shook hands with Brownie and the others I was saying goodbye, and it wasn't easy.

Although I was emotional that afternoon, things were going to get a lot more emotional in weeks to come. For a while Brian Johnston had been coming up to me and saying we should get together to talk about my future. With so many things going on in the club and the game itself, I was more interested in concentrating on playing my footy, so I had never made a time to see him. After the season ended I went away with the boys for a short trip to Cairns and the Gold Coast, then went to see Brian to get my release, the release Geoff Carr had promised.

Johnno is a great bloke and I got along really well with him, but when I went to see him I didn't get the answer I'd hoped for. He said, 'I'm sorry, Gorden, I can't do that.' I said, 'But Geoff gave me his word.' I guess I'm a gullible bloke. If someone gives me their word I believe them, just like I expect them to believe me if I give my word.

Brian just repeated that the club couldn't give me a release and I walked out of his office – and into probably the worst year of my life.

CHAPTER SIX

THE LOST WEEKENDS

When you are out injured, you never really feel part of the team. What I went through in 1996 was about a thousand times worse. When Brian Johnston told me the club wouldn't be honouring Geoff Carr's promise to let me out of my last year I was filthy. Filthy with Geoff for not organising it before he left and filthy with the club for not checking it out and doing the right thing. I spoke to Super League, the Broncos, and my manager, George.

The word from Super League was that their competition was going to go ahead that season and that I should just move up to Brisbane and start training with the Broncos.

The Broncos said they would organise everything and George agreed with me – what was the worst thing that could happen? If Super League didn't get up and running I could just come back to Sydney. I wish it had been that simple. Things turned ugly. Super League and the ARL ended up in court and so did St George and I. Things just went from bad to worse. Actually, that's not entirely true. There was something really good which happened to me that year – meeting the woman who would become my wife. Without her support I don't know how I would have got through it all.

When I arrived in Brisbane, Super League put me up in these flash riverside apartments called Dockside and I started training with the Broncos. There was all this talk at the time, and since, that I was getting paid big money by Super League to sit out that season. That's rubbish. I didn't get paid my football money at all. Super League paid my rent and advanced me a small amount of expenses money from my contract. Other than that I was living on savings. People who reckon I was doing what I did for money should think about that. I had gone from good money in Sydney to next to nothing. I had a big contract upgrade with St George just sitting on Brian Johnston's desk waiting for me – all I had to do was walk through the door. More than that, all I had to do was play football, which is what I loved doing. But there was a principle involved. Saints told me they would do something and then they reneged. I wasn't going to back down, no matter how much it cost me – and it wasn't just the cost in money either. It was emotional as well. Imagine you do something that you love. Something you are good at and get paid well to do. Something you have been doing for as long as you can remember. Imagine that you only have a limited time to do it in. Now imagine that you can't do it for 12 months, and to make it even harder, you have to watch other people do it. I don't think I've ever been more miserable in my life.

Not that Brisbane was a bad club to be around. Just the opposite, which probably made it even harder. Willie Carne lived pretty close to Dockside and he used to pick me up and take me to training. I knew him from the State of Origin team, along with Alfie and Kevvie, Steve Renouf and Mick Hancock, and I knew Wendell from North Queensland. Right from the start they made me feel welcome. Everyone was great, from the players to the back office to the sponsors, which made me want to get out there and play; to show them what I could do and pay them back for how supportive they were being. But all I could do was run around the oval, lift weights and be a tackling dummy for blokes who were having problems with their defence. I'd travel to the games, but when it came time for the players to put their boots on, I'd just go and buy a hot-dog.

To make it worse, whenever the Broncos went down to Sydney I would travel with the team and meet up with all my mates from St George. The other blokes, such as Brownie and Jason Stevens, had started training with Cronulla, and Choc went to Canterbury I think. But when the court case started and it was obvious that Super League wasn't getting up that season, they went back to Saints. I was the only player in the entire game who was sitting it out, and whenever I saw the St George guys they would ask me to come back. They weren't pressuring me, but they couldn't help asking why I didn't just come back until the end of the season. After a bad start the team was going pretty well. There was no bitterness because of the feud, and everyone was earning more money than they had ever dreamed off. They just couldn't understand why I was sitting out, and to be perfectly honest, when I was having a beer with those blokes and laughing about all the great times we'd had, I found it hard to understand as well. There were times when I really struggled. Leaving my Saints mates, who were enjoying their footy as much as ever, and heading to the airport knowing I was going back to being a tackling dummy wasn't easy.

Still, I was always hopeful that things would work out. I don't think I'd ever trained harder in the pre-season, and when we went to Perth for our first trial, I wanted to play so bad it hurt, but the ARL wouldn't let me. That was one of the things that made it so hard. I honestly thought that if I stuck it out, St George would get sick of it and back down. After all, they had my contract money tied up in case I came back. I thought they'd think they could spend that money better on something else. That was the theory anyway. As the weeks went by, Broncos chief executive Shane Edwards and Geoff Carr started trying to work something out. Geoff was working for the ARL by then and he was sort of the go-between. I don't know if that was his job or if he was feeling bad because he'd got me into this mess in the first place, but he was talking to St George and reporting back to Shane. One day, about halfway through the season, we had a breakthrough. Geoff called Shane and said that he'd organised a meeting with the St George board. The feeling we had was that they'd had a change of heart. Shane and I booked a flight to Sydney to go and meet them.

You wouldn't read about it, but the meeting happened at the time when I was finally about to get a game of footy. Somehow Wayne Bennett, through Brad Thorn, had arranged for me to have a game of rugby union for GPS Old Boys, a local club at Ashgrove. Brad's brother played for them and I went down to training, ran a few drills and said I'd be back for the game. When Geoff said the Saints board wanted to see me I dropped everything and headed to Sydney. I've always felt bad about that, because the blokes at GPS probably thought I'd dudded them. If they read this, they'll know what happened.

Actually, the way the meeting went, I probably would have been better off playing for GPS. The board had no intention of letting me go. They thought that if they could get me down there they'd be able to change my mind. Still, at least I wasn't as uncomfortable as Shane Edwards. George picked us up at the airport in his little BMW convertible and drove us to the club. On the way he told us that he'd had a call from Geoff saying that Shane wasn't welcome at the meeting. Shane had to wait in the car. He's a very tall man and he had to spend the next couple of hours squeezed into George's little car. He reckoned he couldn't stand up straight for a month afterwards. George was happy, though – he reckoned Shane was the best car alarm he'd ever had.

Seeing Shane folded into the back seat of that car was the only smile I had all trip. Once in the foyer of the club, George and I met up with Darryl Mather, who I'd asked to be there, and the three of us walked in. Right from the start I knew what was going on. It was an ambush. I'd played for that club for four years and never met one of those directors. Now here they were all over me like a cheap suit, trying to be my best mate. First up I told them my situation. I said I was really happy in Brisbane. My parents had moved down from Townsville to be near me and I'd finally been able to keep that promise I'd made to Mum when I was eight years old, and buy her a house. I was settled and, as a Queenslander, I wanted to be home. They didn't even listen. They'd already worked out what they thought was the solution. They said I could stay in Brisbane but come down to Sydney on Wednesday nights for training. They'd organise a place for me to stay and I could fly back to Brisbane after the games. Again, some people might have taken that offer. After all, it meant I would get paid a lot of money and still get to stay in Brisbane. And it was only for 10 rounds, but as I said earlier, this wasn't about money. To prove that, I made my offer – and I was fair dinkum about it. I said if they gave me a release I would give them my Super League money for the year. Plus they would have had the money from the last year of my Saints contract and the upgrade I was entitled to. I don't know exactly how much that would have added up to, but you wouldn't have got much change out of $600,000. That's how keen I was to play for the Broncos – I would have done it for nothing.

You might think they'd made me a good offer, but I reckon mine was even better. Think what Saints could have done with that money. They could have bought three, four players. They could have strengthened the club for the future. I didn't care what they did with it. They could have all bought themselves new cars or gone on a holiday for all I cared. But they just smiled and tried to get me to come back again. There was one director there, Doug McLelland, who started giving me a speech in this deep voice, using all these big words. It was like, 'Gorden, you've been a credit to this club and a credit to the very institution of rugby league and it is our very deep wish that you confirm your commitment . . .' John Dowling, the ex-Queensland and St George hooker and a bloke who calls a spade a spade, is standing there listening to all this, and he steps in front of the bloke and says, 'What he's saying is, are you f——ing staying or not?' The answer was not. We walked out of there, pulled Shane from the car and tried to straighten him out, and resigned ourselves to the fact that we were headed to court.

GEOFF CARR: I never had any intention of giving him a release from the last year of his contract. I can't think why he would even say that. He certainly never came back to me and said anything about it. I always thought he sat that year out because he had just made up his mind to go. I tried to organise a meeting with St George, because that's what I was doing then. I was working for the ARL and there were a few players who had signed with Super League and gone to other clubs – Nathan Brown, Jason Stevens, Anthony Mundine from Saints. And Matthew Ridge said he would never play another game for Manly, but he did.

They all came back except Gordie, and I spoke to all of them. Honestly, I'm racking my brain, but this is the first I've ever heard of it. I will say one thing, though: if Gorden sat out that year because of a misunderstanding, it is a tragedy. Saints could have won the premiership with Gorden there. He would have had that experience with Saints and then gone to the Broncos. The thought that it might have been because of something he thought I said really upsets me. It's a tragedy.

The case Gorden Tallis versus St George Rugby League Football Club was another lowlight in a miserable year. I was shattered. I had to go into court and be sworn in. It made me feel as if I was a criminal. Honestly, I was terrified. I always felt I was right in what I was doing, but having to sit up there in the box and have this fast-talking lawyer get stuck into me was pretty scary. The thing that really upset me was that it was as if it was some sort of game to the lawyers. We were talking about my life, but it seemed to me they were more keen on sounding good. They weren't even interested in my answers, just trying to lead me into some sort of trap. In his summing up, the judge said he found me to be honest and passionate about what I was doing, so it was nice to get a rap, but it didn't help much in the long run. He found for Saints. He said the club had a binding contract for the season but that they had to offer me my upgrade. They came back with an offer of $1000, which was an insult. I turned it down and that was it.

As well as not being able to play for Brisbane, I now wasn't allowed to train with them, and if I trained by myself, I wasn't even allowed to train in Broncos gear. What I did was put on an old pair of shorts and t-shirt and go for a bit of a run every day. Coincidentally, it seemed that no matter where I went for my run, the Broncos just happened to be training there too. Which was good, because just like before, if anyone had a problem with their defence, the human tackling dummy was available.

It was a weird time. I was part of the club but I wasn't. I hung around with the blokes but couldn't play footy with them. Wayne Bennett was my coach but he wasn't able to talk to me about my game because I wasn't playing. Not that

I was expecting him to pay too much attention to me. I was a big boy, I knew what I'd got into and no-one had twisted my arm. Wayne had a team to prepare and my problems were just a distraction.

WAYNE BENNETT: People don't fully realise what a big thing that was. For a young bloke to sit out a season at the prime of his career, all on principle, is just incredible. He reckoned he'd done his time for St George and they indicated to him that he could leave and that was that as far as he was concerned. They approached him to come back, they did everything they could to get him back but he wouldn't have a bar of it. We didn't put any pressure on him – you can't put pressure on a bloke like Gorden Tallis: he never would have forgiven us. We just left him to do what he thought was right, and he did.

Wayne was friendly and supportive but I never really got to know him that year. That would come later. I was just lucky I had the support of my family and another person who came into my life that year.

I met Christine soon after I arrived in town. At that time Willie Carne was the Hugh Hefner of Brisbane, and he obviously thought I needed some help meeting some of the city's young ladies. One night he rolled by and took me to this restaurant called the Grand Orbit. It was a pretty cool place around town at that time, and if a joint was cool, that's where you would find Willie. This night there was a fashion parade on with all the hot young models strutting their stuff up and down the stage. Willie was in heaven, and he was determined to do the right thing by his new mate. 'What about this one?' he's saying. 'What about this one?' By this time I'd been up to the bar a couple of times and while the models were all pretty, I thought the girl behind the bar was the best thing I'd ever seen. After Willie had pointed to a girl modelling a bikini and said, 'What about this one?' I pointed to the bar and said, 'To be honest, Willie, that girl there is more my type.' I hadn't had the nerve to say anything to her, but Willie being Willie, he walked straight up and said, 'G'day sweetheart. What's your name?'

I stood at the bar and didn't have the nerve to talk to her, but I went back on the Saturday and she was behind the bar again. This time I must have asked her for her telephone number ten times. Eventually she asked the bar manager if she could move to the other end of the bar because I was being such a pest. I didn't give up, though, and finally she said I could call her. I always say she surrendered to my charm. She says she felt sorry for me.

CHRISTINE TALLIS: Working in a bar like that I was always getting asked out, and blokes would ask for my number but I never gave it to anyone. With Gorden I just had to give in because when I kept turning him down he looked so sad I thought he was going to cry. Being a big football star in Sydney, I suppose he wasn't used to getting knocked back. Actually it was more than that. I saw it in his eyes. Gorden's eyes don't lie, and when I said 'no' to him I could see that he was hurt. I remember thinking 'Gee, this guy really means it. He's genuinely upset.' Doing bar work you get used to guys trying to chat you up. It's just something they do when they have a few drinks. It doesn't mean anything to them. Most times they won't even remember it the next day. But Gorden was different. He really did want to ring me. He was sincere, and that made me break my rule.

We went to the movies the first time we went out and it was great to have someone to talk to who wasn't asking me about football or whether I'd be going back to Saints. She didn't have a clue who I was. She asked me what I did for a job and I told her I didn't really do anything apart from playing football. She thought I just played for a local club. The first time she came to my place at Dockside she looked around and thought, 'What does this bloke do? Rob banks?'

At the same time I was finding out more about her. She was working at the bar to put herself through university to be a nurse, and she wasn't a rugby league fan. The only one in her family who followed the game was her father and, as luck would have it, he was a Canterbury supporter and had seen me play my last game for St George against them. The first time we went out, Christine had told him that a bloke who played football was coming around to pick her up to go to the movies, but she didn't tell him my name. When he opened the door he looked me up and down and said, 'Gorden Tallis.

Gee, you're an ugly big bugger, aren't you?' After that we got along great.

Christine was reluctant to go out with a footballer, especially because working in the bar she had seen the blokes like Willie in action, but little by little we became good friends. We'd go out to dinner and to the movies and we went on holidays together to Hamilton Island and Townsville. Seven years after we met, we married.

That night Willie took me to the fashion parade was the luckiest night of my life. I don't know how I'd have got through that year without Christine. She helped put things in perspective and took my mind off what was happening.

Another thing that helped me get through it was my new sporting passion, golf. I'd got into golf about a year before, when I was still at St George. Saints had an old life member named Bill McWilliam who used to be a top golfer. He'd won a few tournaments and had helped Greg Norman early in his career. Bill introduced a lot of St George players to golf, and we started getting out for a hit as often as we could. One person I used to play with a bit was the Dragons' big front-rower Matt Parsons. Believe it or not, Big Matt is a very good golfer, and I lost count of the number of Sizzler meals he won off me that year. It used to drive me crazy. Having played a lot of cricket in my early years I fancied myself as having pretty good hand–eye co-ordination, and the competitive streak kicked in. I reckoned there was no way in the world that a big lump like Matt Parsons was going to beat me, even though I just wasn't in his league. Golf is the hardest game in the world to play, no question. I'd get very frustrated, especially when Matt gave me ten strokes start and still fleeced me, so I got Bill McWilliam to help me with my game. Now it's a big part of my life. I played a lot during that first year in Brisbane. It helped me get out and socialise with the other blokes, and also gave me an outlet for my frustrations. That was the year when I really improved my game, and from there I got to the stage where golf gave me one of the biggest sporting thrills of my life.

In 2001, when I was out with my neck injury, I got an invitation to play in a celebrity challenge at the opening of the Brookwater course just south of Brisbane. I was just recovering from surgery, so I never would have considered it except that Greg Norman was going to be there.

I rang my doctor and said, 'Hey Doc, will I be right to hit a few golf balls this weekend?' He nearly dropped the phone. 'Absolutely not.' I wasn't going to give up without a fight. 'Come on, what about just a little wedge? Only about 100 metres, I'll hardly even tap it.' I was waiting for him to say 'No way', but after a little while thinking about it he said, 'Yeah, I suppose so.' I went out there thinking it would be a little group of us, with maybe 100 people watching. When I got close I got caught in a traffic jam. I thought there must have been a car accident or something, but it turned out to be the crowd trying to get in. There must have been 1000 people there, although it seemed like 10,000. They'd put up these aluminium grandstands and they were packed. It was like the final hole of the British Open. The full course wasn't finished yet so they cut a green in the middle of a fairway, about 90 metres from the tee, and held a 'Closest to the pin' competition. The winner got . . . wait for it, a set of Greg Norman's own clubs, autographed. There was a big group of us – cricketers, Wallabies, TV personalities, basketball players, swimmers, Joe Bugner – who would have been able to punch the ball further than he hit it, plus a couple of newsreaders and one Bronco with a bung neck. We had a bit of a warm-up, and I could see there were some pretty good golfers there, especially the cricketers. I hadn't picked up a club for three months but I was striking them pretty well in the practice.

Then Greg arrived, and Pat Welsh from Channel 7 called us up one at a time and introduced us to the crowd. Then Pat introduced each of us to Greg, who would shake our hand, have a little chat and hand us our ball. Talk about pressure – it told. Everyone, one after the other, duffed it. A couple of the cricketers got onto it okay but they sprayed it wide and didn't get on the green. Then Bruce Paige, the newsreader, got up. I'm not sure if Bruce is much of a golfer, but somehow he hit it along the ground and it wormed onto the green. I was the last one up. I was shaking like a leaf. Honestly, I've never been so nervous. I don't know if it was meeting Greg Norman or the fear of making a goose of myself in front of all those people, but I went to water. I stood over the ball and my hands just wouldn't stop shaking. I don't think I've ever done this before in my life, but I had to step away from the ball because I was such a wreck. I looked at Pat and said, 'Mate, I'll take 50,000 at Lang Park any day; I can't handle this.' Then Greg Norman came over, put his hand on my shoulder and said, 'Come on, how bad can it be? Have a go.' I don't know if The Shark managed to filter some golf vibes into my body or what, but I went back, stood over the ball . . . and hit the best shot of my life. From the moment I connected I knew it was there. There was a bloke down on the green with a microphone and he was calling it all the way: 'This is good, it's straight for the pin, it's a winner.' It landed about half a metre from the pin. Winning

Origin or a Grand Final, and leading your country out for a
Test match are all thrills you can't even explain properly, but
doing that with Greg Norman watching was a thrill all on its
own. I've still got Greg's clubs, of course, it's just that I've
never had the nerve to use them, and I probably never will.

So those were the things that got me through my year on
the sideline: golf, my family and friends, and Christine. But
it was still a very, very long season.

After Saints lost the Grand Final to Manly, Choc Mundine
came up to join the Broncos and we all went to the United
States together for the end of year trip. Choc was my roomie
on that trip and it was great to be spending some time with
him again. I know some people don't like Choc; they say he is
a lair and a big-noter and all that, but I'll bet you they've
never met him. I'm not going to go in to bat for Choc Mundine – he doesn't need my help – but I will say this: anyone
who knows him doesn't have a bad word to say about him. He
comes out with all that stuff in the media to build up his pro-
file and sell tickets to his fights, and he does it knowing it will
rub some people up the wrong way. Choc's philosophy is that
if people who don't know him badmouth him, what does it
matter? They don't know who he is. I know who he is and I
like the guy. He's a good mate who always calls to see how
things are going. When my father had a stroke a while back,
Choc was always on the phone. I just wish other people could
see him the way I do and realise what a champion bloke he is.
When he arrived at the Broncos, no-one really knew how to
take him; luckily, we had that trip together, and we all got to
know each other really well. The only disappointment was
when we were in Las Vegas and ran into Jeff Fenech. He said
he could get us some tickets to the first Mike Tyson–Evander

Holyfield fight. They were $300 each. We thought Tyson would knock Holyfield out in 10 seconds, like he did every-one else he'd fought, and we didn't want to waste our money. We went to the weigh-in, along with about 15,000 other people, but left before the fight to go to an NFL game in Denver. Needless to say, we missed one of the all-time great fights.

Still, I'd just finished my own big fight and I was looking forward to finally getting back on the field. After a year not playing and spending a lot of time lifting weights I had gone from 98 kilos to 115 kilos, so I knew I had plenty of work to do in the off-season, but I've never been happier to do the work in my life. I'll never forget the first time I finally got to run on for the Broncos. Up until then the only coach I'd had was Brian Smith, who was the most meticulous coach you could ever have. Brian would write a game plan about how he was going to write the game plan. Nothing was left to chance, from the way you tied your bootlaces to where you stood for the kick-off. Before each game you would get a dossier on every opposition player. It would be something like 'Darren Lockyer, right hand carry, left foot step, prefers high ball to grubber . . .' and there would be instructions like 'first ruck you go to second marker, third tackle drop behind left centre'. Everything was very structured, and I just assumed every coach would be like that.

Before our first game, against Auckland at ANZ Stadium, I went up to Wayne and said, 'What do you want me to do?' He said: 'What do I want you to do? Go out there and play footy. That's what we're paying you for.' It was the best thing I'd heard for a year.

CHAPTER SEVEN

WAYNE'S WORLD

I reckon Wayne Bennett's greatest strength is his ability to pick people's personalities. He works out who you are and what will motivate you, and then he pushes your buttons. These days at the Broncos we work with a sports psychologist named Phil Jauncey. Phil works with the Lions, the Bulls and the Australian Olympic team, and knows all there is to know about what goes on in an athlete's head. He gives us these tests to work out what sort of people we are. There are all sorts of categories: mosquito, feeler, enforcer, thinker. I'm a mosquito-enforcer, which means I buzz around annoying people, but when the time comes I'm prepared to take someone on physically. With that information Phil is able to work out the right way to make me achieve the most I can. But the thing is, Wayne Bennett never needs any psychological tests to know what sort of person someone is. He knows from speaking to you and looking at the way you are around the club or on the field: from that he knows how to treat you.

As far as Wayne is concerned, everyone is different, so he coaches the individual. He doesn't expect everyone to have the skills of, say, Darren Lockyer, and he doesn't expect everyone to relate to the words that would motivate, say, Shane Webcke. The way he treats me is totally different from the way he treats Locky, Wendell, Alfie or Kevvie. He knows that if he had spoken to Wendell the way he speaks to me, Wendell would probably have reacted differently from the way I did. Or that if he spoke to Alfie that way Alfie would just laugh at him. Every player is different, so every message is different.

He knows I'm a passionate bloke and that I run on emotion a lot of the time, so when he says something to me before a big game, something to really fire me up, he knows he has to go straight to the heart. I remember the first game I played for Australia. When something like that happens you can't help but think back to when you were a kid and how you always dreamed of wearing the green and gold jersey. I know my brother and I would always play footy in the yard after watching a big game on TV and we'd fight over who would get to be Wally Lewis. Well, before I ran on for Australia the first time, Wayne just walked up to me quietly and said: 'Gorden, make every kid want to be Gorden Tallis tomorrow.' It sure worked for me.

It took me a little while to find out all this about Wayne,

because for the first couple of weeks of playing for the Broncos, he hardly said a word to me. He was known as the best coach in the game at the time, but for a while I couldn't work out why everyone had such big raps on him. I thought, 'This bloke's having everyone on, he's just a coach and he doesn't even tell you much.' I know now that I was used to Brian Smith's style of coaching, where no stone is left unturned. Wayne's style is different, and knowing what I had gone through the previous year, he knew the best way to bring me into the team was to give me some time. I hadn't played for a season, my weight was up, and basically I was off my game. I was playing all right, but nowhere near the standard I wanted to be. I was trying to fit into a new team and, of course, I was trying to do everything at a million miles an hour to make up for lost time. Wayne stayed away from me because he didn't want to put any more pressure on me. It was only when I started to catch up in terms of match fitness that he started to tell me what he wanted from me. And that was when I began to realise what a wonderful man he is.

Wayne believes in helping his players on and off the field. I remember not so long ago I was talking to him and I mentioned Phil Jackson, the basketball coach of the LA Lakers. I said, 'Imagine how hard it must be for Phil Jackson. His two best players, Kobe Bryant and Shaquille O'Neal, hate each other.' He told me that he believes coaching blokes is more about what happens off the field than about what happens on the field. That's why he is so keen that everything is going well in your personal life, whether it be your relationships with your family, or your finances. I have to admit, I found that a little hard to take at first. One of the first times I was in his office he sat me down and just asked me, straight out, what I did with my money. I remember thinking that it was a pretty personal question but I answered him anyway, and he said if I ever had any problems to talk to him. I know he was worried about what everyone was going to do with all the extra money that came into the game after Super League. That was when everyone stopped having outside jobs; Wayne wanted to make sure it didn't become a problem. It was around then that he arranged for the TV investment guy Paul Clitheroe to come in and talk to us about shares and term investments and all that. Another time he made us all do a computer course. We all had to sit in a classroom with a teacher. I think we were the worst class ever. Alfie was sneaking around pinching everyone's disks and turning off the machines when we were in the middle of something.

While Wayne's interest in our lives away from the club might seem a bit personal, it makes good sense. He believes that if we are organised, know how to manage our time, have our business affairs all sorted out and are happy in our personal relationships, it will mean we can do our jobs as footballers more effectively. As he says, you only spend 25 hours a week with the football team. That leaves about 140 hours a week, and if you are happy for the 140, you will work harder for the 25.

It works both ways. Wayne tries to make the team like a family as well, and if you have problems outside the club you can draw strength from the team. I know that is how it was when Kevvie went through the worst thing that could ever happen to anyone. Just before the 1997 season, Kevvie and his wonderful wife Kim learnt that Kim had breast cancer. Wayne called us all in and told us what had happened. He didn't tell us how to react, just the facts, and that Kev and

Kim needed our support. For most of us that meant treating Kev exactly as we always had, making sure that the time he spent with the team was as much fun as it had always been. After Kim passed away early in 1998, I read an interview where Kevvie said that being with the team had been his escape. It helped him get away, and when he went back to his family he was better able to help Kim and his three boys.

To Wayne, team and family are the most important things, and the way you mix the two is the key to everything. You only had to see the *Australian Story* program he did to see how Wayne is with his family. He is an example to all of us of getting the mix right. I must have had 100 people come up after that program and say, 'I never liked Wayne Bennett before, but after seeing that show I reckon he's great.' Of course it was nothing new to us; we've known that side of Wayne for years, but he hides it from the media. There are some people who believe that Wayne doesn't speak to the media very much so that when he does have something to say it will have more impact. Maybe, but I think he just doesn't care about them. I asked him about it once and he said, 'It's not my job to sell newspapers, it's my job to coach a football team. If my team goes out and plays a great style of football, that's promoting the game. That's how I talk to the media.'

Because he isn't comfortable in the public eye and is often pretty short with interviewers, the public has the impression that Wayne is a quiet bloke who never has a laugh. That's not right. He thinks he's the funniest bloke in the world. I get sick of his jokes all the time, I wish he'd shut up. Actually, I must admit, he can be pretty funny at times. His favourite name for me is 'Kettle', because he reckons I run out of steam early. He'll come up with these one-liners at training which break everyone up. The other thing about Wayne is his incredible physical fitness. Every year we do this pre-season run around the reservoir at The Gap, which is about 10 kilometres up the road from our training ground. It is one of the hardest things you could ever do. The first ten minutes absolutely kills you – it is 1.6 km straight up hill. I remember the first time I did it, I had only been going about three minutes and I was asking myself some pretty serious questions. They reckon The Gap run can either make you or break you and that's absolutely right. Before I got to the club Shane Webcke had arrived; he was this big overweight kid from the bush. They reckon he set a record in The Gap run – for the slowest time. The only person to beat it was Sorb Lavea, this 135 kilogram forward who walked in off the street in 2003 asking for a trial. He got lost on The Gap run and our trainer had to go into the bush in his four-wheel drive after about two hours to search for him. He found him sitting under a tree praying. He was a giant of a bloke but he was scared stiff of the little green frogs hopping around everywhere. He told Kevvie Walters afterwards in his big, deep voice: 'It was like a Hollywood movie. When I saw the headlights, I knew I was saved.' Webbie didn't take two hours, but it was close, and I'm told there were some people in the club who didn't think he had much of a future. A couple of times in his first season he got knocked over in a game and it looked like he wasn't going to get up. Webbie decided he was either going to make a go of it or go home, so he headed for The Gap run, on his own, in the pre-season. Once he beat The Gap run, he could beat anything, and anyone. By the time I got to the club he was a gun, with huge raps on him. So when I say The Gap is a tough run, believe me. It has broken a lot of people, but it has never beaten Wayne Bennett. When we run it, so does he, every year. The bloke is in his fifties but he still finishes in the top five of The Gap run every year. He just won't give up, and when you have a coach like that, it challenges you. I hate to say it, but even at his age he can beat me in a one km run at training. He'll sidle up beside me with that silly crooked smile of his and say, 'Come on Kettle, let's see what you can do', and no matter how hard I try, he'll always beat me, bugger him.

Another thing with Wayne is that even though he's a winner, he doesn't have a huge problem with losing. As long as the team has given everything it has, he's happy. In 2001, when we were going through a shocking run and losing by a couple of points here and there, he never got up us. He just kept trying to work on the positives. He could even laugh about it, hard as it was that year. There was one game against Cronulla down in Sydney when we got beaten, and Alfie and Kevvie went out and had a big one all night. The Bee Gees had that song 'Tragedy' that went, 'Tragedy, when the feeling's gone and you can't go on, it's tragedy'. Well Alfie and Kevvie got on the bus and were singing 'Tragedy, when your halfback's stuffed and your five-eighth's stuffed, it's tragedy'. We were singing it all the way to the airport, and even Wayne had to smile. It was only when he felt we weren't putting in that he got angry. There was a game against Melbourne that season when we got absolutely flogged – the worst loss in the club's history. It was about 20 or 30–nil at half-time and Wayne really gave it to us in the dressing room. He reckoned the passion and commitment weren't there and he was right. But if we've tried and lost he's fine. In fact, some of the best speeches I've ever heard Wayne give have been after losses.

In 2001 we lost the Grand Final qualifier to Parramatta 24–16. I was out, Ben Ikin was out, Scotty Prince was out, and so was Carl Webb, we'd had all that controversy about Justin Hodges getting sacked, and Wayne just said the team had played well and he couldn't have been prouder. With him it's not always the result on the scoreboard that's important; it is what the boys have put in, or as Wayne says, that we have 'paid the price'.

Early in 1997, Wayne didn't have any problems with my effort. It was just the execution that was letting me down. The problem was I was just trying too hard and my body wasn't ready. The first game I got to play that season was for Australia in the World Nines in Townsville. The tournament was the first event put on by Super League after the court ruled that they could start their own competition, and Australia played against USA in the opening match. I probably didn't deserve to be there, not having played the previous season; I think they chose me more as a reward for what I had been through than anything else. Not that I could care less about how I got there. I was just pleased to be back on the field. I was determined to wipe out 12 months of frustration as fast as I could. The first time I got the ball, a couple of seconds into the game, I just went for it. It didn't matter how many big Yanks there were in front of me – they were never a chance to stop me. I burst through and scored next to the posts, so you could say I was the first player to score a try in Super League, and given that I was the only player to sit out the season, that was probably fair enough.

I can't put into words how good it felt to be playing footy again. An added bonus was to be playing in Townsville. I was also pleased that I could finally show Christine what I did for a living, although I think it took a little while for her to get used to it.

CHRISTINE TALLIS: Over the 12 months since we had met, I had got to know Gorden as a kind, gentle person. Obviously I was interested to see this guy I had been dating for a year play football. I'd heard all this stuff from my dad about Gorden being the super-sub and how he'd been well known down in Sydney, but I had no idea. I have to say it was a shock. You could only describe him on the field as being the complete opposite of the Gorden I'd got to know. These days I'm used to it, but I still can't see how a genuinely soft person can be such so aggressive when he plays football.

The first time I got to wear a Broncos jersey was a trial match against North Queensland in Port Moresby. You've never come across anyone who loves rugby league as much as the Papua New Guineans. You couldn't set foot outside the hotel without getting swamped, but the person they really wanted to see was Alfie, because he was as small as they were. We ended up calling him the 'Albino Kumul' because we reckoned he looked just like them, he was so small and has that little flat nose. I was determined to put on a good show, so I went out to have a look at the ground before the game. I soon realised we were going to be playing on a field of bindii. Not that it wor-ried me – I just wanted to get involved. I tried to take the ball up every play and do every tackle myself. At 9 o'clock that night I was still pulling the bindiis out of my backside. When we tried to get on the bus after the game we were absolutely swamped by all the fans trying to touch us or shake our hands. The police were belting them on the head with these sticks but they just stayed there, so out came the dogs. You should have seen those New Guineans sprint away when the rottweilers arrived. Willie Carne couldn't have caught them. By the time we got on the bus there was still a big crowd. Wayne Bennett stood up and told us to take all our gear off. Everything – boots, jerseys, socks, shorts, the lot. We were all sitting there in our jocks and Wayne said, 'Now give it to them', so we handed everything out through the windows. You should have seen their faces. I reckon a few of them would have got mugged on the way home but you've never seen happier people than those kids walking off with Alfie's jersey and socks.

After that it was all downhill. As I said, I was so far off match fitness, and just as it always is after a long lay-off, the harder I tried the worse I went. Still, at least I had the support of my new team-mates. Well, most of them. Wendell Sailor has to be the biggest sledger of all time. Early that season, when I'd arrive at training after a match he'd say, in front of everyone, 'Orr gee, mate, you're the most overrated player I've ever come across. Mate, fair dinkum, give back the car. How can you drive around in that car? Holden must be spewing. Mate, ring up Reebs, give back the money. How can you look at yourself in the mirror?' He also had this thing he'd do where you walked into a room and he'd pretend not to see you and really give it to you. He'd be talking to someone and saying stuff like, 'Mate, what about Tallis? How overrated is he? If I was a selector I wouldn't even have him on the bench.'

Then he'd see you and go, 'Oh Gordie, didn't see you, mate, how ya goin'?' I got used to it after a while and besides, it wasn't just me he'd be doing it to. He'd give it to everyone. Even Darren Lockyer got the 'Mate, give back the car' routine at one stage in his career. He was a real character, Wendell, and I loved playing with him because he was such good fun and a great competitor. He'd talk all the trash-talk, but no-one tried harder on the training paddock and you knew he'd put in on the field. It didn't always come easy to him. Wendell was an athlete, but he wasn't a natural footballer like, say, Lote Tuqiri. Lote was born knowing how to draw a man, put a bloke through a gap or beat a tackle with an in-and-away. Wendell had to learn it all. You had to take your hat off to him, because he never lacked confidence and he was willing to back himself. When he got to the club the wingers wearing the Broncos numbers 2 and 5 were Willie Carne and Mick Hancock, who just happened to be the Queensland and Australian wingers as well. That didn't stop Wendell going out and getting a BMW with the numberplate 2BMW5. You had to love the guy.

The way he got to the Broncos was through winning one week's training as player of the carnival at some junior event in North Queensland. He arrived and trained the house down. He was always big and strong, and he'd win all the 400-metre sprints and looked great. Kelvin Giles was the Broncos' trainer then. He'd trained the English Olympic team and his background was in athletics, so he knew an athlete when he saw one. He went in to Wayne and said, 'This kid Sailor is a great athlete; he could be anything.' Wendell was only about 18. Wayne hadn't met him, and nobody had seen him play, so Wayne called him in to his office and said, 'They tell me you're a great trainer, but can you play?' and

Wendell said, 'Orr yeah, Benny, I can play, mate, don't worry about that.' He never changed.

When Wendell left the Broncos to go to rugby union it was a real blow to me. I wanted to keep playing with him, and thought we'd play out our careers together, especially after he'd told us he was going to stay. We were over in Leeds having a drink the day after playing the World Cup final at the end of 2000, and Wendell told me, Webbie and Locky that he was going to sign with a club in England and play league and union when his contract ended at the end of the next season. It was a pretty emotional night. We'd just played for Australia in a winning side with Wendell man of the match. We had a great team at the Broncos – we had just won the comp and reckoned we could win the premiership for years to come, so we all tried to talk him out of it. By the end of the drink we were all rock solid. We were going to play out our careers with the Broncos. There had been plenty of speculation about what Wendell was going to do, so we got on the phone and rang Wayne in Brisbane. It must have been about three in the morning, Brisbane time, but he came on the phone and Wendell told him what he'd just told us, that he was going to re-sign with the Broncos. Then I got on the phone and Benny said something like, 'You blokes have a special bond. You're all lucky to have each other.' Then we let him get back to bed and we went back to the bar.

After that we flew back to Brisbane for Michael De Vere's wedding, then Christine and I went off to the US for a couple of weeks. I'd always wanted to go to Disneyland, and at the age of 28 I shouted myself a trip. When we were in Hawaii on the way back I rang Mum and she said, 'Wendell's going to rugby union.' I told her it was just paper-talk and not to take too much notice, but when I got back I turned on the TV and sure enough there was Wendell saying he couldn't decide whether to go to the ACT Brumbies or the Queensland Reds. I couldn't believe it. He rang me the next day and said we had to go out for a coffee, and that's when he told me his reasons for going. I accept them. I never begrudge a bloke trying to set himself and his family up, so I'm fine with it. I just wish he'd stayed from the point of view of the Broncos, and also because we had so much fun together. That last season didn't pan out the way he would have liked, because we didn't send him out with a Grand Final win, but we did have that special night when we won the first Origin and no-one can take that away from him. I wish him well, even if I do call him 'The Judge' because he spends so much time on the bench for the Wallabies. He always used to wear this gold and diamond number 5 around his neck – I am still convinced it was cubic zirconium. When he went to rugby he told me that he was going to buy a number 11, which is the winger's number in union, but my number in league. He thought that was great. 'Hey Gordie,' he said. 'This will be good. I'll be able to swap you my Wallaby jumper for your Kangaroo jumper because the numbers will be the same.' I said to him, 'Thanks Wendell, but I don't think that will work.' He asked why not and I said, 'Because we don't have number 22 in rugby league.' Funny thing, he wasn't laughing half as much then as he was when he was saying I should give my car back.

Luckily I never did have to give that car back in 1997, because after about ten games I started to come good. We had a game against the Hunter Mariners down at their home ground, which we lost, but me and Choc really clicked. The Mariners were a good side no matter how much the Newcastle Knights supporters tried to put them down. They had

Brett Kimmorley and Scott Hill and were well coached by Graham Murray. They gave it to us that night, but I had one of my better games that year and Choc and I started to get a bit of the old St George combination going. When I walked off I really felt it was finally starting to come together.

WAYNE BENNETT: I realised the sort of player he was little by little, as part of that slow process. He took a while to come back after the year off but he always had those eyes, those cash register eyes. I've only ever coached two players like that; the other one was a bloke named Jack Casey, and he was beautiful too. I loved him, but he had to give it away early. You always know with blokes like that, when play time comes and the eyes start rolling – you know to look out because something's going to happen. More importantly, the opposition knows too.

Soon after the Mariners game we played Wigan in the World Club Challenge and I got into a blue with their forward, Terry O'Connor. I reckon I'm better known in England for that one fight than for anything I have ever done on the field for Australia or the Broncos.

He was a big lump of a bloke who thought he was tough and spent the whole night belting me around the head. That's the way the Poms play. We grow up saying 'they can't run without legs', but they think it's 'they can't run without heads'. After one head-high too many he pushed me in the play-the-ball, I thumped him, we had a bit of a punch-up and Bill Harrigan sent us to the sin-bin – the first but not the last time Bill would show me the way to the sideline. We won 34–nil, but to read the papers the next day you'd think the only thing that happened was the fight. I'd managed to land a few before he got his first one in. His first was a goodie, though – the first time I'd seen my own blood in all the years I'd been playing the game. Unfortunately, it was on TV, and everyone replayed it about 20 times. There was even some retired doctor who rang up Super League and said I could have killed him. Terry O'Connor didn't seem to think so. He said his wife could punch harder than me, which only made me happy I was fighting Terry and not her.

GLENN LAZARUS The Sunday Mail, *22 June 1997: I was second marker when Gorden Tallis and Wigan's Terry O'Connor got stuck into each other at the play-the-ball in Monday night's World Club Challenge match at ANZ Stadium. To say I was stunned at what took place is an understatement. You don't see much of that sort of thing in the game these days, where two blokes land so many clean punches on each other.*

Usually, when the first punch is thrown players from both sides come from everywhere and start grabbing each other and the matter is resolved without too much drama. The other night we saw two hard men having a go at each other, and while it might not have been pretty, it is a fact of life that league is one of the toughest sports around and occasionally when blokes lose their cool they are going to come to blows. We know when we take the field there is a risk of injury, even permanent injury, and we know that sometimes we might have to put our fists up.

A couple of people have voiced their opposition to what has happened, but the fact is the players concerned have forgotten all about it – for the time being anyway.

About six weeks later we had to play Wigan again, on their home ground of Central Park, and all anyone could talk about was how Terry O'Connor had said he would fix me up when he got me on his home turf. To tell you the truth I was really looking forward to it. I'd promised Wayne I'd behave myself, but the thought of playing over there in front of a big crowd screaming at me really fired me up. Unfortunately, it never happened. We played Canberra the night before we left and I hurt my back. It was the sort of thing that normally would not have stopped me playing the next week, but after sitting on a plane for 20 hours and then a bus for a couple more, it seized up. We were staying at this place called Mottram Hall, which was an amazing old castle with its own links golf course. The ARL boys could bag us all they liked, but I'll say one thing for Super League, we always went first class. This place was fit for a king. Pity Wally Lewis wasn't playing with us any more. The physio had got my back right and I went out for a game of golf and everything seemed fine. I even eagled the ninth with all the boys watching from the balcony, which I was pretty happy about, but then when I bent down to put my tee in the ground on the tenth, my back went again and that was it. I was ruled out. When we got to Central Park it was just like old times for me. The boys went to put their boots on and I went to buy a hot-dog. Didn't the crowd give it to me. 'You gutless booger, you're scared of our Terry', 'Terry was going to give it to you, ya soft bustard.' I bought my hot-dog and got back to my seat as quickly as I could. It would have been some game if I'd played.

As it happened, I didn't even get to see the end of it. I was at the hospital with Glenn Lazarus. Glenn had been my roomie since the start of the season – his old partner Kerrod Walters went to Adelaide and I took his spot. I couldn't have asked for a better person to learn from. Lazzo was a winner. To win one Grand Final is a great achievement, but to win five, with three clubs, as Lazzo did, is just amazing. Wayne had asked John Ribot when he was Broncos' CEO to bring Lazzo to the team when they just didn't seem to be able to break through for that first premiership win. They had a lot of talented players, but what they wanted was someone with NSWRL experience who knew how to win the big games. Wayne had worked with the young Lazzo when they made the 1987 Grand Final with Canberra, and knew what a winner he was. Lazzo had won two premierships with the Raiders by then, and when Reebs managed to bring him across, he turned out to be the missing ingredient. For me to end up rooming with someone like him was just another one of those lucky stepping stones in my career. Like Brian Smith and Rod Reddy and Wayne, he was just what I needed at that time. I get asked what it was that Lazzo had and others didn't, and I say it was just the presence of the bloke. Some people call that arrogance but I call it confidence. Players like Lazzo have ability, but they have also done all the hard work that makes them secure in their ability.

For a big bloke to do what Lazzo did in a game was incredible. I always used to say that he was a small man trapped in a big man's body. He'd do 23 hit-ups in a match and come across in cover tackles – all the things that a bloke his size just shouldn't be able to do, and everything had a real quality about it. Much as he would have liked to be a five-eighth or a centre, Lazzo knew he was a front-rower and he didn't overplay his hand. He just did his job, and did it better than anyone else. I remember playing against him for St George at Kogarah one day. Brian Smith was very big on statistics, and he'd make sure he got the stats for the opposition as well as his own team. This day the Broncos had beaten us and Brian had the stats in front of him and he said: 'You want to know what you have to do if you want to be the best? Well listen to this . . .' Then he read out Glenn's stats for the game. I only remember him doing that for one other opposition player, and that was Terry Lamb.

As far as I was concerned, Glenn was like another coach. When we went away for a Saturday match we'd be watching the Friday night game in our hotel room and he'd point out things like, 'See the way that bloke is running? He's going a bit too sideways, they'll push him back here', and you'd listen, because no-one was better at making an extra 10 metres than Glenn Lazarus.

That night in Wigan was the game when Glenn broke his ankle. It was one of the most horrible things I've ever seen. His ankle turned right around so that his foot was sticking out at this weird angle. I went in the ambulance with him and the big bloke was in a lot of pain. Then when we got to the hospital they stuck him behind a curtain and no-one came near him for 90 minutes except for this nurse who stuck this giant needle in his leg. I can't believe he didn't belt her. It was only when our team doctor arrived after the game that he got any treatment. The lesson to be learnt from that is never get injured in England. Their health system is the same as their cricket team, not up to scratch.

It was a great trip, though – my first time in England. Our second game was against the London Broncos, and when we'd been in London for a day John Plath told me he'd been to have a look at Piccadilly Circus. I said to him, 'The Piccadilly Circus, where is it?' He told me it was a couple of stops on the train and that he'd been and seen all the monkeys and elephants and clowns in their little exploding car. I said I was really looking forward to going and all the boys joined in, telling me about the great bear act they had there. When I got there I was disappointed that it was just a big street with lots of buildings – but at least I gave the boys some entertainment for a few days.

We ended up winning just about everything that year. The premiership against Cronulla, the World Club Challenge against the Mariners and the Tests against England and New Zealand. The only thing we didn't win was the Tri-Series final, but at least it took NSW the longest game in history to beat us. I don't remember a lot about that 103 minute game apart from being bloody tired at the end, but there is one incident that occurred during the series that I'll never forget. We were in Auckland for the game against New Zealand and the boys were all out having a drink and relaxing in the hotel bar a couple of days before the match. I was playing air hockey with Alfie and the puck got caught in the hole at the end of the table. He put his hand in to free it up and cut his finger. It's not like he slashed it open or anything. There was just a little bit of blood, but he looked at it and walked over to Wayne and said, 'Wayne, you've got to get me out of here, I'm going to faint.' I laughed, because I thought he was joking, but sure enough, he keeled over and hit the deck. And he was out like a light. Wayne had to pick him up and get him to his room. We couldn't believe it. Here is one of the toughest players in the game, a little bloke who has never let a big bloke get over the top of him, and he's terrified of the dark and can't stand the sight of a little bit of his own blood. Still, we didn't let it put us off our preparation. One of the trainers had some black electrical tape in his pocket so we put on some black armbands and kept drinking.

That Tri-Series was typical of the whole season. As much as we tried to say it was the same as Origin, it wasn't. We were playing for Queensland against NSW, but the jerseys were different, and most importantly, we knew that some of the best players weren't playing. NSW was probably harder hit than us. They still had Ricky Stuart and Laurie Daley and Brad Clyde, but they didn't have The Chief Harragon or Brad Fittler or the Johns boys, and to really feel that you were playing at the top level, those players had to be there. Same with the premiership. We were saying it was Best of the Best but we knew we were playing in half a comp – and so was the ARL. It was a great experience to play the Grand Final in front of a record crowd at ANZ, and to be able to celebrate with our fans in Brisbane that night instead of catching a plane home, but until we beat the Newcastles or Manlys or St Georges we knew we couldn't really call ourselves the best team in the game – and neither could they.

We'd get our chance. Sooner than everyone expected.

CHAPTER EIGHT

YOU WIN
SOME . . .

I remember sitting in front of the TV at home watching
Newcastle win the 1997 Grand Final over Manly. It was a
strange feeling to be watching a Grand Final as a spectator,
but it was a strange year. It was a good game of footy, and I
was barracking for Newcastle, but I still felt that something
was missing. Looking back on it now, I think that's how the
public was feeling too. You wouldn't have had too many
complaints from Newcastle supporters that day, but really I
think everyone had a bit of a hollow feeling throughout that
season. Not the players really – I know that after sitting out
the year before I was just excited to be back on the field – but

you could tell from the crowd figures that the split in the game was turning people off. I guess people don't like change, and there was always the question of which competition was the best. We had that sensational Tri-Series final against NSW, but our Grand Final wasn't too hot because of the weather. They had a great Origin series with Fatty's No-Names beating Gus's All-Stars, and their Grand Final was good because the underdogs got up to beat Manly. I didn't know it until I moved down to play for the Saints, but everyone in Sydney has two favourite teams – their own and whoever is playing Manly – so the Knights had a lot of support that day. I enjoyed that game because of the result, but the thing I remember most is Adam MacDougall stamping on Geoff Toovey's face and getting away with it. I couldn't believe he wasn't sent off, but I guess the ARL didn't want to spoil the occasion.

Of course after we'd won our Grand Final and the Knights had won theirs, there was a lot of talk about holding a 'Superbowl', with the Super League champions up against the ARL champs. It would have packed any stadium in the country but it was never going to happen. We all thought it was because the administrators of the two comps hated each other too much to consider it, but in reality it was because they were working on a much bigger plan – getting back together.

When that happened, before the 1998 season, the Superbowl became a reality, but not as a special match. The Broncos would meet Newcastle all right, but it would be at Marathon Stadium in Round 8 of the premiership. Believe it or not, we don't really get excited about 'big' games at the Broncos. We try to approach each match the same way, no matter who it is against, but that game against Newcastle was one time we made an exception. It was the first time two Grand Final teams from the same year had met, and I reckon both teams were playing for more than the two points. It really meant a lot to us, and the game set the tone for the entire season. We had gone into the year as premiership favourites, but until we played Newcastle there was always going to be a question mark over us.

It was a great night for us. It had been raining all day so the ground was heavy with mud, which didn't worry me one bit. That meant it was going to be a real forward contest; both packs were ready to get stuck into it. You really couldn't have set it up better: Marathon, a heavy track and a sell-out crowd. I reckon if you asked every player in the competition if they could have anywhere except their own ground as their home ground they'd all say Marathon. The crowd there is just fantastic. They scream and yell and really get behind their team, and that just fires everyone up. That night in 1998 was one of the best. The media had really built it up, and there was a real buzz around the ground – it all went off like a firecracker. I remember Chief Harragon and Shane Webcke giving it to each other from the kick-off. The best thing, as far as we were concerned, was the way Darren Lockyer played. He'd had a bad night for Australia against New Zealand a week earlier and was being blamed by the media for losing the Test. Given that it was his first Test, the bagging he got could have shattered the young bloke's confidence but it didn't – Locky is a class act. He went out in one of the biggest club matches of all time, in front of a screaming crowd, in pouring rain, and had a blinder. I think he got a couple of tries and was kicking goals from everywhere. That was one of those games when you look at a bloke on the field, shake your head and think, mate, how can you do that?

Actually, I found myself doing that quite a bit in those first couple of seasons with the Broncos. Seeing Alfie Langer sprinting flat out in one direction, then just stopping, propping and heading off again at another angle while everyone else is grabbing air. Or the pace and balance of Steve Renouf. I loved playing with Pearl. You always knew that if you could get him a little bit of space he'd score. He was so good, but so modest about it. And Lazzo. Teams all practise trying not to get turned on their backs these days, because it is such a big part of the game. Lazzo didn't need to practise any sort of wrestling moves; he knew what to do. I don't think he ever got turned on his back in his life. Those are the sorts of players who make a champion side, the once-in-a-lifetime players like Gasnier and Raper and Langlands at Saints or Sterling, Kenny, Cronin, Price at Parramatta or Daley, Stuart and Clyde at Canberra.

You get plenty of good players and good teams, but they'll never take that last step up unless they've got a couple of great players in the side. It's not that the great players win games, although they will always pull something special out when things are tight; it's the fact that great players make the good players around them play better. How many times have we seen a good player from a middle-of-the-table club get picked for Origin and play a blinder? That's often because that player has to do everything for his club side. He has to run the team, make all the breaks, call all the moves, do all tackling. But put him in a top side with good players around him and all he has to do is concentrate on his own game.

And there is another thing, too. Everyone wants to think

LEFT: Mum used to say to us, 'Look after each other. You're all you've got.' My big brother Wally and me with our 'minders', Robyn (left) and Jannita. I was about four years old and the photographer had to give me the little pig to stop me crying.

BELOW: First day at preschool. In the middle of the second row. Nothing's changed.

CURRAJONG
STATE PRE SCHOOL
GP 4
1978

RIGHT: We'd do anything to get into a footy jersey. Me and Wally as ballboys when Dad was coaching Souths in Townsville about 1978.

BELOW: Finally getting a game. Central's Under 8s, 1981. I'm standing in the third row, third from right.

LEFT: The 'cheeky Murri from Townsville' and my mate Nathan Brown.

BELOW: My last year with Saints, 1995. We played Wests at the Sydney Cricket Ground in a replay of the 1963 Grand Final.

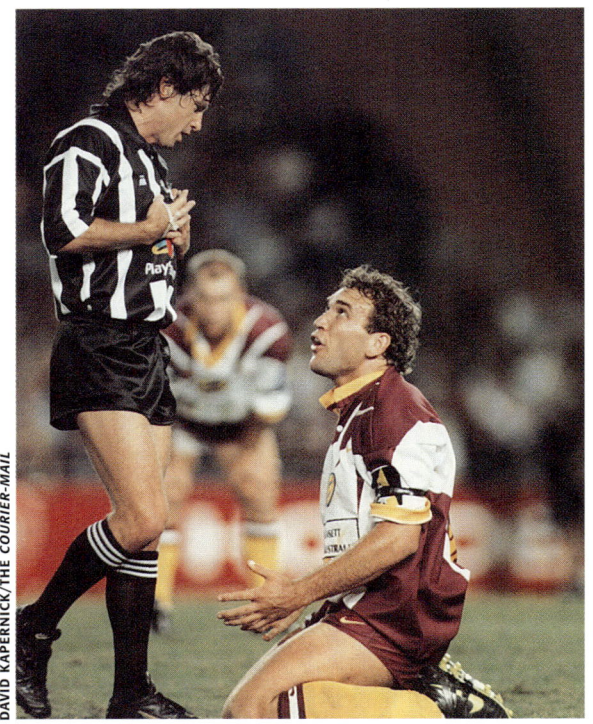

'Bill, honest, it wasn't me.' Bill Harrigan and I have an early difference of opinion during the Super League competition in 1997.

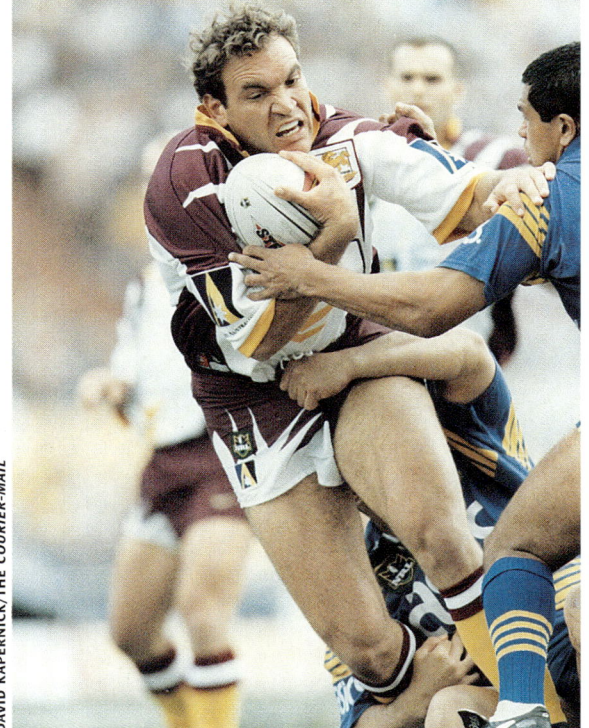

I love playing Brian Smith's sides. John Simon tries to tackle me for Parramatta in 1998.

A long way from Canungra. Craig Wing goes low and Ryan Cross and Dallas Hood come in to help in the 2000 Grand Final.

Sharing a moment with our captain Kevvie Walters after winning the 2000 Grand Final. It was supposed to be Kevvie's last game but like his mate Alfie, he couldn't stay away.

Bringing home the trophy in 2000 with Kevvie and his son Jett.

The Broncos' new captain with my vice captain Darren Lockyer at a city promotion before the 2001 season. I wouldn't have the job long before Lockie had to take over for a while.

ABOVE: 'You haven't got the balls, Bill.' Guess what? He did. Bill Harrigan sends me off in Game I, 2000.

RIGHT: Game III, 2000 – the one I said we shouldn't play. With Paul Bowman and Jason Hetherington after I'd scored in our humiliating 56-16 loss.

Celebrating in the dressing room with Lockie and Wendell in early 2001 – one of the few games before my neck injury.

My favourite picture. Leading out Queensland as captain for the first time. Suncorp Stadium, Game I, 2001.

Happy or what? Celebrating Chris Walker's try as we win back pride in Game I, 2001.

Photo - David Kapernick
The Courier-Mail

The try I scored when I was 'unconscious' after being hit by Penrith's Scott Sattler in 2002. Those are his legs on the right.

DAVID KAPERNICK/THE COURIER-MAIL

ABOVE: Alfie's last Origin. A draw in Game III, 2002, was good enough to send him out a winner.

LEFT: Winners are grinners and the shield comes home with us.

NEWS LIMITED

DAVID KAPERNICK/THE COURIER-MAIL

Beyond my wildest dreams, captaining Australia against the Kiwis on October 12, 2002.

On the spot reporter. From left: Matt Giddley, Steve Menzies, me, Hazam El Mazri, Trent Barrett and Darren Lockyer after we beat New Zealand in 2002. (Taken with my camera.)

RIGHT: A jersey to be proud of.

BELOW: Spot the tennis player. Pat Rafter joined us for a training session in 2000.

Photo-David Kapernick
The Courier-Mail

RIGHT: Wayne Bennett . . . he knows the right buttons to push. I just wish he'd lay off the jokes a bit.

BELOW: With two of the all-time greats, Alfie Langer and Wally Lewis, at the Broncos Annual Ball after winning the 2000 premiership. Wayne Bennett was with us but managed to hide from the camera.

DAVID KAPERNICK/THE COURIER-MAIL

BOB JONES

RIGHT: Our faithful hound, Tyson the Wonder Dog, as a pup.

BELOW: More nervous than before Origin. With Greg Norman after I won his clubs.

Photo-David Kapernick
The Courier-Mail

LEFT: A perfect day. Mr and Mrs Tallis outside the chapel on Hamilton Island . . . Christine left me speechless. That's her mum Monica Egan on the left and my mum Judy on the right.

BELOW: Team Tallis. From left: Judy, Wally, Mum, Dad, me and Jannita. Still as close as ever.

that they belong in top company, so they lift themselves to
the level around them. When I first came to the Broncos
Lazzo invited a few of us out to his house one day. I went out
there and couldn't believe it. It was a mansion. Everything
was top of the line. We were sitting out on the balcony, over-
looking the floodlit tennis court, and out comes the gold
cutlery. I was eating pizzas out of cardboard boxes at the
time, so to say I was impressed doesn't come close. I don't
know if it was all put on for our benefit, but I remember
thinking, 'So this is what you can get if you get to the top in
this game'. It was the same when I went on the field with
blokes like Lazzo and Alfie and the rest. I wanted them to
think I belonged. If I had an aim back then it wasn't necessarily to play Origin or for Australia. It was just to be noticed
by the really good players. I wanted them to be able to say to
their kids, 'I played with Gorden Tallis. He was a good
player.' That was the goal; everything else followed from it.

It wasn't just team-mates, either. I also have real respect for
some opposition players. You play against them for your club
and if you are good enough you will play with them or against
them at Origin and international level. Generally, you get to
know them and like them, and even when you are playing
against them you can have some fun on the field. Blokes like
Joey Johns will always have a laugh, especially back in the
days when his brother Matthew was playing with him at
Newcastle. They were a bit like Alfie and Kevvie; they knew
each other's game so well and would really chatter away to
each other. When they were running hot they would do this
thing where they wouldn't call for the ball, they'd bark like
dogs or moo like cows or make bird calls. I know it sounds
juvenile, but it was really just a couple of blokes loving what

they were doing and having the time of their lives. Of course you'd always try to beat them, and if you got your hands on them you'd want to hit them as hard as you could, but we were still mates. I remember one game we played against the Knights at ANZ. It was late in the game and somehow I got the ball off the back of the scrum. I drew in Robbie O'Davis and gave the ball to Locky, who scored next to the post without a hand laid on him. It was ridiculously easy, and when I was walking back I passed Joey, who was headed under the posts. We looked at each other and just burst out laughing. It was like, 'How arsey was that?' He is a cheeky little bugger, Joey. In one Origin match he was giving it to our young forward John Buttigieg. When John got the ball Joey'd be yelling out, 'Run at me, you big fat cheesecake.'

Of course Wendell was another one who had plenty to say on the field. When Wendell was on fire there was no shutting him up. He'd be bursting onto the ball and calling out to the opposition, 'Here comes big Dell boys, you can't stop me today. Big Dell's too strong for you. Oh yeah, I love it . . .' There was one game at WIN Stadium against St George Illawarra where Wendell was absolutely unstoppable. That was the one that started all the talk about him going to rugby union, because it was the day after Jonah Lomu had scored the winning try in the Bledisloe Cup game that they called the best rugby union match of all time. Wendell scored an amazing try against the Dragons which had everyone wondering how he and Lomu would go against each other. I think that's what got Wendell all excited.

You've got to give it to him, that was some try. There was some young kid marking him and they both went up for a kick about 10 metres out from our line. Wendell took the ball and shrugged the kid off, then bumped off someone else and headed off up the field. The kid had another go at him but Wendell brushed him off again and ran 90 metres for the try. Later on the kid got the ball and Wendell cleaned him up over the sideline and got up yawning, as if it was all just too easy. Then he called out to their captain, Trent Barrett, 'Fair dinkum, Bazza, put someone else on will ya, this bloke's our best player.' It was pretty cruel I suppose, but that was Wendell; once he got on top of someone, he liked to grind them into the ground. He was always saying stuff like, 'Who is this bloke?' or 'Someone get me a program, I have absolutely no idea who this guy is' when someone tried to tackle him. With Wendell, the mind games started when he arrived at the ground and didn't end until he went to sleep at night.

But annoying as Wendell could be if you were playing against him, the biggest pest in the game would have to be Jason Stevens. He's the one who's giving the wedgies and grabbing you on the crotch, then going and writing all these books about being a Christian and not having sex until he's married. The way he's always sticking his hands in your private parts, I don't think it's the Christian thing that is keeping him away from the ladies. I think he needs to have a good think about his preferences. Actually, I'm only kidding. Jason's a great bloke and I enjoy playing with him and against him. In fact, he reckons if he gets stuck into you it's a compliment. If you complain when he grabs you on your privates he just gives you this big smile and says, 'Mate, I wouldn't do it to you unless I liked you.'

You forget a lot of the sledging that goes on, but some of it just sticks in your mind. I remember one year at St George when Tony Priddle was playing front row for us. Tony was the professional's professional. He used to do all the stuff like protein drinks long before anyone else, and he was fit as a fiddle. We were playing the Roosters and Bruce Sinclair knocked Tony out with one punch. It was a lucky punch, but Tony felt pretty bad about it because he prided himself so much on his strength and fitness. Anyway, word got around. The next week we were playing the Gold Coast. That was the year Craig 'Tugger' Coleman had come back from England, and he was having one last season with the Coast. Every time a scrum packed down Tugger said to his front-rower, Dave Woods, in that little stutter of his, 'Hey Wood Wood Woodsie, go easy, mate, don't pack pack down so hard, you'll knock him out, you'll knock him out.' Finally Tony had had enough, and told him to shut up, and Tugger said, 'Hey hey watch it, dickhead or I'll knock you out myself – and then you *will* be embarrassed.'

Of course, there wasn't any of that amusing stuff going on that night when we played the 'Superbowl'. It was as hard a game as you could play, and a very, very good game to win. We won by 20 points, and while I know a lot of ARL supporters would say it didn't prove a thing, it certainly meant a lot to us.

That night pretty well set the platform for our year. Once we beat Newcastle we were hot favourites to go all the way, but as always, the big stumbling block was going to be Origin. With so many Broncos in the Origin team the way we recovered from the series would be crucial. For once everything went our way.

For me it was a special series, because it was the first time I had played since 1994. A lot had happened to me since I was the green kid who sat in the bus too nervous to open my mouth. I'd settled in at the Broncos, played in the Super League rep games and knew the senior blokes like Alfie, Kevvie, Pearl and Darren Smith well. Plus Wayne was coach, so you could say I felt right at home. More than that, though, for the first time I really thought I had earned my spot. That first time, when the lady in the hairdressing salon told me I was in the side, was like some sort of dream. This time was different. Whenever anyone is chosen to play for Queensland they are made to feel part of the side. That is part of Queensland's strength. There is no divide between the blokes who have been around for a while and the newcomers. Once you're in, you're in. The only difference is the size of the contribution you make. In 1998 I felt ready to make that contribution. Once again, the only problem I had was getting on the field.

Remember how I said I would never have been cleared to play by the judiciary in 1994 if I hadn't been with St George? Well, guess what? I was in trouble before the 1998 series, too. The difference was, this time I was playing for the Broncos and this time I didn't get let off. I was cited to appear for striking Cronulla's Martin Lang after I'd tackled him. I was trying to flop on top of him to keep him from getting up for a quick play-the-ball but somehow I missed and clipped his head with my forearm. I pleaded guilty and Wally Lewis and Steve Roach appeared for me, asking for leniency so that I could play Origin. The judiciary ruled that Origin was worth two club games and suspended me for three games instead of four so I could play in the second Origin match. And who replaced me in the side? Martin Lang. At least he had a blinder, but it was still hard sitting at home watching the match on TV. That was the game where Kevvie Walters kicked ahead on the second tackle with about a minute to go. I nearly threw the remote control through the TV I was so angry. I was screaming, 'Kevvie, what are you bloody doing?', and then Ben Ikin ran through and regathered and Tonie Carroll scored the try which Locky converted on the bell for the win, and I'm saying, 'Great kick Kevvie, you're a genius.'

The second game I came into the side and the Blues flogged us. I'd played three games over four years and still hadn't been on the winning side. But that's the thing about Origin. You can play at your absolute best and win by two or lose by two and then play at 95 per cent and get beaten by 30 points. That's how good the players are; if you're not absolutely at peak performance, you'll get hammered. Luckily, we were at peak performance in Game 3. Out of all the games I've played in my life, I reckon that's the most perfect match I've ever been involved in. I'm a bloke who never comes off the field entirely satisfied. I'll always think I could've done better or be angry about something that I know I didn't do the way I should have. But from a team point of view that night was probably as close to the ultimate game as I'll come. Our completion rates, the way we followed the match plan, everything just went like clockwork. And like I say, when one team is 'on' and the other is just slightly 'off', anything can happen. Plus we had Alfie at his best that night, and when that happens you're always going to be very hard to beat. I know it must be getting boring the way I rap Alfie, but what else can I do? The bloke is amazing. He has these tiny little hands – actually, I've always thought that he is really a dwarf – but somehow his passes are always spot on, and he'll just do things that if you hadn't seen them with your own eyes, you wouldn't believe. That night, with about 15 minutes to go, the Blues committed the cardinal sin and held off him. He had the ball about 10 metres out on the last tackle and they thought he was going to kick. He dummied to kick once and they held off a bit, then he dummied to kick again and they held off again, and by then it was too late. He ran between Brad Fittler, Tim Brasher and Matt Johns to score the try that won us the series. At last, the monkey was off my back.

I have to give Wayne a big rap for that series. Fatty had done a great job since 1995 but it was always going to be hard to pull the ARL and Super League players together in 1998. I wasn't involved in 1996 but I heard there were a few problems between the players, and in 1997 we were split into two different comps. So whoever had the team in 1998 was going to have to be more than a coach. He had to be a peacemaker as well. Wayne's way of handling the problem was typically Wayne. He just concentrated on beating the Blues. We were a team, no Super League or ARL, just Queenslanders – most of them from the Broncos. That gave us a big advantage. All our moves were Broncos moves; nearly the entire backline was the Broncos backline. All Wayne had to do was slip the players from the other clubs into a system which was already working very smoothly for the Broncos. Needless to say, he did it without any fuss.

But to me one of the best things about winning that series was that when it was over, everyone was talking about Steve Renouf's defence. There had always been this talk that Pearl was a good club player but in Origin his tackling let him down. That's the thing about Pearl. You wouldn't see him winning the 400 metres sprints at training – wouldn't see him winning anything at training, as a matter of fact – but when you really needed something special, he was the man. That's how he was that series, and it wasn't through his attack, although that was as good as ever: it was his tackling. He shut up a lot of critics in 1998, and that's always great to see.

As I said, after Origin we just seemed to stay on a roll. The replacement players had done a great job while we were away, which meant that we weren't trying to catch up on any dropped points, and the run in to the semis was relatively easy. We beat Wests by about 50 points in our first game after Origin and didn't lose again for the rest of the minor premiership. The closest we came was a draw with Balmain, so for the last six weeks or so we were really just waiting for the semis to start. When they did, it was Parramatta first up at ANZ, and we ran out thinking all we had to do was show up. Did they prove us wrong or what?

Brian Smith had worked out some master plan to upset our momentum by kicking into touch and not letting us get a roll on. You have to hand it to him, it worked. They beat us 15–10 and thought they had our number. In fact the only ones who had beaten us were ourselves. We thought we were going to win the competition easily and our intensity had gone off. We paid the price, but losing to Parramatta that day was probably the best thing that could have happened to us. It would have been a lot worse if we had realised we were off the pace on Grand Final day. As minor premiers we still had a second chance, and we made the most of it. Nothing much was said in the dressing room after the game. We knew what was wrong and we knew what we had to do about it. I put it all down to attitude. You can talk about it all you want, but the only one who can change it is you, and that side was experienced enough and good enough to get back on track.

The next week we went down to Sydney, where we were too strong for Melbourne. We weren't back to our best, but we were good enough to score six tries to one and set up a Grand Final eliminator with Gus Gould's Roosters. When I think back about my all-time best memories, this game was one of them. I never really care about who is coaching a side that we play against. You don't tackle or run at the opposition coach. To me they aren't really part of the equation, but there are two coaches I do notice.

Now as I've said, Brian was very good to me when I was at St George. I think he is a very clever coach and he played a big part in making me the player I am, but that doesn't mean I don't love beating him. Same with Gould, who is another very good coach. I've had my differences with both of them, so beating a side coached by Brian Smith or Phil Gould is very special. I don't know what it is about them, all I know is that beating a side coached by Brian Smith or Phil Gould is very special.

And it's not just me, either. There are a lot of players who feel like that. I remember that after we beat the Roosters in the 2000 Grand Final, Gould had a go at us on radio. We were back at the club the next day, having been celebrating long and hard, when someone came up and told us that Gould had said that we hadn't really won the premiership. He reckoned it was more that the other teams had underachieved. What a load of crap. If they underachieved it was because we didn't let them achieve. You go out and watch any

143

team at training and they all look like world-beaters. All their moves work, their wingers can run a million miles an hour and the forwards are ferocious. Then you put them up against a side which belts them in the tackles, smashes it up the middle and puts pressure on the halves and all of a sudden they are underachievers.

Still, what could you expect? Gus had coached the Roosters for five years and never got them to the Grand Final and then Graham Murray took over and got them there in his first year. What was Gus going to say, that we had beaten a hot Roosters outfit? Better to bag us and them in the same sentence. We weren't happy about it, but we could have copped it. It was when he singled out Wendell for a serve that we really jacked up. As I said, we had been celebrating pretty hard and were feeling no pain, so when some bloke came up and told Big Dell what Gus had said about him, he asked the bloke if he could get Gus's phone number for him. I don't know how he got it, but somehow a few minutes later we had the number and someone was ringing Gus on his mobile. I have to give Gus credit – he laughs about it now. He was on the golf course, and Dell just gave him a gobfull. It was like, 'What would you know about it, you wanker, how many winning Grand Finals did you play in?' Then the phone got passed around and everyone had a go. Someone yelled out, 'Hey Gus, when are you going to give the pig its head back' and then Kevvie started up the chant that you always hear when you play them at the Sydney Football Stadium, 'Roo-sters clap clap clap, Roo-sters clap clap clap'.

But that was still two years off when we played Gus's Roosters in 1998. They came up to ANZ thinking they were finally going to get to a Grand Final, for the first time in 23 years, and we absolutely smashed them – 46–18, nine tries to three. With 15 minutes to go we had them down 40–6. It was the greatest number of tries ever scored by the Broncos in a final, and Locky got three of them. To make the weekend even better, the next day the Bulldogs knocked Parramatta out of the running after the Eels had led them 18–2 with 11 minutes to go. Once again one of Brian's teams had choked. You almost had to feel sorry for him. Almost.

The Bulldogs had pulled off two miracle come-from-behind wins to make it into the Grand Final, but we had a plan. We let them lead us 12–10 at half-time so they couldn't come from behind. That's our story, anyway. We piled on 20 unanswered points in the second half to set up a 38–12 win. Tonie Carroll had a blinder, but somehow I ended up winning the Clive Churchill Medal for best player. I'm still copping a hard time about it from some of the blokes. I agree with them, there were other players who deserved it more than me, but I'm not giving it back. It's in the bottom of my sock drawer. One day I might wear it around my neck like Eminem with all his chains.

Actually, I find the whole concept of the Clive Churchill Medal a bit strange. How can you give it to one bloke when so many players got you to the game in the first place? We wouldn't have even got to the Grand Final if it wasn't for the replacement players doing so well when we were playing Origin. Still, at least I was in good company. I reckon the best player hardly ever wins it. The year I got it Tonie Carroll was the one who really broke their back in the second half at a time when the game could have gone either way. I can honestly say that of all the blokes I have ever played with, no-one has ever been able to change a game as quickly as Tonie Carroll. He can do it with one big hit or one big run, and he sure did it in that Grand Final, even though it didn't win him the Clive Churchill Medal. The next year Melbourne's Brett Kimmorley got it, but the player who won that game for them was Tawera Nikau. The Storm were down by 14 points at half-time and Nikau came out after the break and went berserk. If Nikau doesn't play, Melbourne don't win. Same in 2002. The Roosters Craig Fitzgibbon won the medal, and there's no denying he had a big game, but in my opinion the man who made the crucial plays was Freddie Fittler. If Freddie doesn't play, the Roosters don't win. I've asked Joey Johns when he's going to give back Ben Kennedy's Churchill Medal for the 1997 Grand Final. He's said as soon as I give back Tonie Carroll's. Still, it's all history, isn't it? As we said to the Bulldogs that afternoon, just look at the scoreboard.

DAVID MIDDLETON Rugby League Yearbook 1999 *Players of the Year: He has been described as rugby league's 'Raging Bull' and adjectives such as terrifying, unstoppable and awesome invariably appeared in print before the name of Brisbane second-rower Gorden Tallis.*

Tallis was awarded the Clive Churchill Medal after Brisbane's 38–12 Grand Final win over Canterbury and in his next game – the second Test – he was again named man of the match.

Two instances of Tallis' belligerent style emphasised the difference he made to a Brisbane pack that in times past had been less than aggressive in its approach. Against Newcastle in May's

*'Superbowl', he performed two crunching tackles on the Knights'
forward leader, Paul Harragon. First he picked him up and drove
him into the ground, and later his crunching tackle forced
Harragon to lose possession. Then, in a hard-fought contest against
St George at Kogarah Oval, Tallis turned game-breaker when he
scattered defenders like ninepins to score the decisive try late in the
game.*

*Tallis was both menacing and brilliant in the second Test against
the Kiwis. It was his first Test in a united Australian team and the
combative atmosphere suited him perfectly.*

*The second-rower with the fire in his eyes was devastating at all
levels of the game in 1998, and if Wayne Bennett is any judge,
Gorden Tallis is only going to get better.*

That night we flew back to Brisbane in a specially chartered
Ansett jet. It was just the players, partners, family and sponsors. The players and their wives and partners sat up the
front. They put the replay of the game on the screens and it
was really nice to sit there quietly and reflect on what we had
achieved because once we landed at Brisbane Airport we
didn't get another quiet moment for a long, long time.

The thing is, I remember sitting on the plane that night
with Christine and thinking how well everything was going.
We had a sensational team, we all got along so well, and the
future was looking bright. Alfie was wisecracking and jumping around, looking as fit and happy as a 12-year-old. I don't
think I've ever felt closer to a team of blokes in my life. I
looked around at the players on that plane as we laughed and

raised a beer or a glass of champagne and thought, how good is this? Who's going to stop us? If you had told anyone up the front of that plane what was around the corner, we wouldn't have believed you.

CHAPTER NINE

. . . YOU
LOSE SOME

When I started thinking about writing this book I asked Wayne Bennett if he could suggest a story which summed up Alfie Langer. He told me to tell about how Alfie retired in 1999 because he couldn't bear to let anyone down. He's right. The way Alfie walked away from the game he loved because he thought he was letting the rest of us down says it all. The thing was, we didn't think Alfie was letting us down. We knew that would never happen because Alfie always gave everything for the team, but in his mind, he wasn't pulling his weight. He thought he was dragging us down.

It was a strange day when Wayne told us that Alfie was

retiring. The thought of the Broncos without Alfie was something we'd never really considered, because he was such a big part of the place. We thought he'd be there for as long as we were and then some, but that day reality hit home, and the Broncos wasn't the same team any more. It meant more than replacing a player or changing the way we played football; it meant a big part of us went too. It was weird.

But that's just the sort of year it was. Weird, very weird. Like I said, if someone had told me on that flight after we'd won the Grand Final that within a few months we'd win only one of our first ten matches or that Alfie would have quit the club, I'd have called the flight attendant and told him to check what was in the champagne. Still, incredible as it was, that's exactly what happened. Sometimes during the first few months of the season I'd find myself shaking my head and saying, 'What the hell's going on?'

Everything had been going so well. For me it started when Wayne came up to me a few days after the Grand Final win and told me I was going to be named in the Australian Test team to play New Zealand. You wait all your life to hear those words. I had played for Australia before, in the Super League side which won a three-Test series 2–1 against Great Britain in 1997, but this was something else again. I would never downplay that Super League series. We had had some of the best players of all time, like Laurie Daley, Brad Clyde, Andrew Ettingshausen, Wendell, Locky, Webbie and Steve Walters, and we were playing against the full Great Britain side, but as with the Tri-Series, you couldn't help feeling it wasn't quite the real deal.

But the team in 1998 wasn't as strong as it might have been, either. Australia had already lost the first Test in the series earlier in the year, and now that the club season was over a lot of the top players were having surgery on niggling injuries. The players who took their places were good, but inexperienced. Locky was playing his second Test after copping a lot of flak for his performance in the first one, Steven Price, Darren Britt, Ben Ikin and I were all coming into the side. On top of that, Bobby Fulton had stood down as coach because his wife was sick and Wayne had stepped in. It wasn't the way I imagined it would be. I thought if I ever got into the Australian side there would be blokes like Brad Clyde and Freddie Fittler and Laurie Daley there, and Bozo would be the coach. I thought I'd be learning the tradition of the side from them. But here I was, surrounded by players who hadn't played a lot for Australia before, under Wayne, who hadn't coached Australia before.

We were staying at the Heritage, the flashest hotel in Brisbane – probably one of the flashest in the country. It had TV sets in the bathrooms. The food was sensational and we were pampered, treated like rock stars. The night of the Test we all got dressed up in our R.M. Williams-sponsored shirts and trousers and boots and headed down to the meeting room before catching the bus to Lang Park, feeling pretty good about ourselves. When we were all sitting down, Choppy Close, who was team manager, stood up in front of us. 'Look at you,' he said. 'To a man you're wearing $1000 worth of clothes.' He waved his hands around the room. 'Look at the joint you're staying in. It's a mansion. Well, you listen to me, fellas. Some of the blokes who represented their country before you were lucky to get a pair of khaki shorts and a rifle. They didn't stay in any fancy hotels. They slept in rusty, tinny boats for weeks at a time to do their bit for

Australia. Only they weren't playing any game. They were going to war.'

Now I'm not much of a believer in motivational talks, but this really hit a nerve with me and it still does. When I play for Australia I don't just think about the green and gold jersey, I think about the slouch hat. I once saw a show on TV where all these old soldiers were talking about what they had been through in the wars, and one old bloke said, 'The only reason they called us "Diggers" was because the deeper we dug the more chance we had of staying alive.' I've never forgotten that. I'm not saying what we do is anything like what the Diggers did. I know we are playing a game, but I like to think of the sacrifices the soldiers made and how they did their bit for Australia. It's hard to put it into words, but playing for Australia is different from anything else. You mightn't know the blokes around you as well as you know your teammates in club footy or feel the atmosphere as much as you do in a packed stadium on Origin night, but to be one of 17 blokes chosen to represent your country on a given day is an amazing feeling.

That night at Lang Park was when Wayne came up to me and said that thing about making every kid want to be Gorden Tallis. Those words, and the slouch hat, are the two things I always carry with me when I play for Australia.

CHRIS ANDERSON, Australian coach: Gordie's a very passionate player, and playing for Australia suits him. I suppose some people take to it more than others, but Gordie is like all the senior blokes who have played for Australia for a while. They love pulling on that jersey and being looked upon as the best in the world. They want to play at that level, and why wouldn't they? Gordie took to it from the start. He loves to play with passion and what better place than playing for your country?

Running out to play my first Test at Lang Park was something I'll never forget. I knew my family was there in the crowd. I always think playing in a game like that isn't just a reward for all the hard work the players put in; it's a reward for the parents too, for the hundreds of hours and thousands of litres of petrol they've spent taking their kids to matches and practice over the years. So to look down and see yourself wearing a green and gold jersey, well, it takes some beating. We won that game in Brisbane pretty convincingly. My main memory is having a real good tussle with Jarrod McCracken. He was big and hard – just the type of player I love playing against. You give some and cop some.

With the series all tied up, we headed over to Auckland for the decider. You know the Kiwis can always lift themselves for a big one. They have been knocking off Australian sides in New Zealand for years. Things didn't get off to the best start when Kevvie pulled his hamstring mucking around at training, but Matthew Johns came into the side and went well. So did Steve Renouf, but the real match winner for us was Alf, who was captaining Australia for the first time. After the match, with everyone singing and spraying champagne and having a great time, I remember looking over and seeing

Wayne and Alf sharing a quiet moment together. It had been quite a year – the first time anyone had captained or coached a side which had won the premiership, Origin and a Test series all in the one year. Alfie always used to give Wayne a hard time about the fact that he had wanted Laurie Spina and not him when he made his Origin debut in 1987. He was always saying stuff like, 'I wasn't good enough for you back then, was I?' but that night in Auckland they had gone just about as far as you can go.

That was the last time Wayne ever coached Australia, which I have always thought was ridiculous. I asked him about it once and he gave me some answer about wanting to give up something that was important to him, which I still don't understand. I think it was one of those tests he gives himself. It was like he had everything he'd ever wanted as a coach and he wanted to give something up to prove to himself that he could. Maybe it was a way to keep his feet on the ground. I don't get it. All I know is that he did a great job as Australian coach and he should do it again.

We left Auckland on a high. Wayne and Alfie were at the top of their games, we had the premiership and Origin safely in Queensland and we were looking forward to another clean sweep. How wrong could we be?

How does a team which won the Grand Final pretty convincingly go straight to being a team which can only win one of their first ten matches? I still can't give a good answer to that one. All I know is that in our first ten games, the only team we beat was Souths. We came close plenty of times, but we just couldn't seem to click into top gear. If anything was going to go against us in a tight finish, it would, and try as we might, we just couldn't seem to turn it around.

It started in our very first game, against Canberra at Canberra. With half an hour to go, Ben Walker was sent off for a head-high tackle. It didn't look anything too bad to me, but the linesman thought differently. We shouldn't have been laughing, but with Alfie it is sometimes hard not to. Ben had stuck out his hand and caught the Canberra player high. Referee Tim Mander had seen it and stopped play and the linesman ran in to get his face on TV. Alfie went over too, and when the linesman said to Tim, 'It was serious', Alfie said with a straight face, 'So it was serious, was it?' The linesman goes, 'Yes, it was very serious, Alf.' Alf goes, 'Oh, very serious.' Tim Mander says, 'So it was serious?' and Alf said, 'Very serious.' 'Yes,' says the linesman, 'very serious.' Alfie is geeing them both up and by the time he finished there must have been about 10 'seriouses'. Unfortunately, Tim thought it *was* very serious and sent Ben off, and we lost 28–20. The next week we went down by eight points to Cronulla. Wayne could accept the loss to Canberra and he could accept the loss to Cronulla, but it was the loss the next week to Melbourne at ANZ which really upset him.

We went out that day expecting to win but got hammered 48–6 – the worst defeat in the club's history. We weren't to know that Melbourne would go on to be premiers, but there was no excuse. It was Lote Tuqiri's second game, and the first time they kicked it to him he let it bounce and they scored. So they just kept kicking it to him and he kept letting it bounce and they kept scoring. I remember just standing there with my mouth open, watching the ball go over my head. By the end of the game my tongue was sunburnt.

Poor Lote. After about half an hour Wayne took him off. As it happened he called me off for a breather at the same time. I didn't know Lote was behind me and the crowd started booing him. I was thinking, geez, I'm not playing that bad, am I? It was the sort of debut that could wreck a bloke for all time, but Lote came back better than ever. By the time he left the club to play rugby union he was the crowd favourite at ANZ.

We didn't have a win in 1999 until Round 6, against Souths, then we had just a draw and three losses in our next four games. The week after we beat Souths we played Melbourne, and even though we didn't win, I managed to get in the headlines again when the Storm's chief executive Chris Johns blew up about me sledging Rodney Howe. I knew Rodney well. We'd played in junior rep teams together and he was a bloke I had some respect for. He was in the group of players who had all come through at the same time and were known as pretty hard men. As I said at the beginning of this book, no-one gets a reputation like that easily. You earn it, and once you have it, you fight to protect it. But when I found out that Rodney Howe had cheated the system, that his reputation was 'wind assisted', as I call it, I lost respect for him.

I played against Rodney in an Origin game in 1998. He was everywhere, taking the ball up, knocking blokes over, and he never slowed down. He was like a tank, with bullets bouncing off it. He just kept coming. One time he got the ball and I hit him with everything I had. I really wanted to hurt him, but it was like hitting a concrete wall. My whole side went numb and I felt physically sick. Kevvie was firing me up, telling me what a good hit it was, but I was worried. My theory is that if I'm hurting then the bloke I've just hit is hurting too, but that night I just felt like I was hurting, but he wasn't.

When the news came out that he had been busted for taking the steroid Stanozolol I remembered that night and thought, 'Right, so that's what it was. He cheated us.' He was out for close to a year and he came back in that game against us in 1999. I'd been thinking about it a bit, and when I was getting ready for the game I said to Wayne, 'I'm going to give it to Howe today. I'm going to have a go at him.' Wayne said, 'What happens if he comes back at you?' I said I didn't care, I'd handle it, and he said something like, 'Well, you're a big boy.' When we were getting ready for the kick-off I called out, 'Hey boys, look, Stanozolol's back. Watch out he doesn't jab you with his needle. G'day, Stanozolol.' He looked at me and his eyes were like saucers. He couldn't believe it. Before he'd got busted he was respected as one of the hardest men in the game. No-one would have spoken to him like that then. As he was jogging to the first scrum I called out, 'Here comes the Chemist, boys. Come on Chemist, hurry up.' He just looked at me and said, 'Run at me, run at me.' So I did. The first time I got the ball I ran at him and he hit me. I could feel that he wasn't the same. Without the drugs, he was just a player. I heard he was pretty emotional in the dressing room after the game. Chris Johns stormed into our room to complain to Wayne. Wayne just told him not to bother him, so Chris went to the papers. Rodney and I are fine now, we've done a few promotions together and get along well. As far as I'm concerned, he paid his price and I let him know how I felt. He has accepted that, so that's the end of it.

That game was another loss, but there were signs that we were coming back. I think Wayne always thought we would come good. After all, this was pretty much the same side that had played the year before and won everything on offer. We were working hard at training and, most importantly, we were still a team. One thing about a team which is on the skids – and I don't think it matters what sport you are talking about – is that it starts to break up off the field as well as on. Blokes start getting round in little groups of two or three, and when that happens, they start griping. The groups begin talking about each other behind their backs and looking for someone to blame. Once you get that 'team within a team' business, you're gone. That didn't happen at the Broncos that year – Wayne wouldn't let it, and more importantly, neither would we. Matter of fact, in a funny sort of way, losing like that week after week brought us together and made us stronger.

Up until that year the worst losing streak in the Broncos' history was four games. When we lost nine out of 11 no-one could believe it, but nobody was hurting as much as Alf. Alf was our most senior player, and our captain. He led from the front, of course, but there was more to it than that. For over ten years, whenever the Broncos had needed something special to pull them out of a hole, Alfie had provided it. This year he was trying just as hard as ever, but the magic acts weren't happening. It hit him hard. As I said earlier, Alfie would do anything for the team. If you told him he had to be at training at 6 o'clock in the morning to run 20 km cross-country, he'd look at you as if you were nuts. If you said the team needed him to do it, he'd be first one there. To feel that he was letting us down – for the first time in his career – just ate away at him.

It came to a head in Townsville the night we played the Cowboys. Alfie loved playing footy more than just about anyone I've ever met. Once he was on the field you couldn't get him off with a crowbar. From time to time, if we had the match won Wayne would send one of our trainers on late in a match to get Alfie off the field. It might have been to give some young kid a couple of minutes' experience or because Alfie had played a rep match a few days earlier, but either way Alf didn't like it one bit. Most of the time he told the trainer to get off and leave him alone – in not so many words. But that night at Townsville was different. We were behind and Wayne pulled Alfie off because he wasn't having the impact a fresh player could have had. I don't think that had ever happened before in Alf's career. You just didn't take Alfie Langer off unless you were well in front. After all, if there was any way the game could be won, Alfie was the one who could find it. But this night Alfie was taken off and Ben Walker went on. Then in the last seconds of the game Ben kicked a miraculous goal to give us a draw. When we scored a try, which brought us within two, no-one else wanted to take the kick, but Ben couldn't get his hands on the ball quick enough. He was so full of confidence and enthusiasm. He really wanted to be in that pressure situation and he did the job.

That night we were having a drink at the bar after the game and I noticed there were tears in Alf's eyes. I went up and asked him what was wrong. I thought there must have been something wrong with a member of his family or something. That's how inconceivable it was to me that Alfie might have thought his career was over. He told me everything was fine and that I shouldn't worry, but later I saw him talking pretty seriously with Kevvie. A few weeks earlier they had been sitting on the bus singing 'Tragedy', but there was no joking that night.

When we got on the plane to head home we knew something was wrong. When we travel, the players always sit down the back and Wayne sits in business class. This time Alf sat up front with Wayne. They must have had a long talk all the way back, because when we got together for training on the Tuesday, Wayne sat us down and told us Alf had hung up the boots. Alf had been too emotional to tell us himself, and who can blame him? I can't even imagine how much he must have been hurting.

The thought of footy without Alf was very hard for all of us to contemplate, but there wasn't anything we could do about it. I always thought the club should have just put out a statement saying that Alf had a groin strain or a hamstring tear and given him six weeks to think about it, but that wasn't the way it happened. Alf was gone and we just had to get on with the season. Thanks to all the hard times we had been through, we were closer than we had ever been. Even before Alfie had left we were starting to improve, and from the Cowboys match on we began to turn it around. We set two records that season: a five game losing streak and an 11 match winning streak. As I said, it was a weird year.

There were highs and lows on the representative scene as well.

I only played the one Test match, the Anzac Test in Sydney, which turned out to be Alfie's last game for Australia, but we made sure he enjoyed it. We had one night at an Italian restaurant called Beppi's. Alfie was in good form. On those nights, with the ARL paying, Alfie always takes it upon himself to order the wine. He grabs the wine list and it's like, 'What have you got, what have you got?' Alfie wouldn't know a good wine from tap water, but he always manages to order the most expensive and then, when it comes, he goes through the whole routine, sniffing it, rolling it around in his mouth before saying, 'Ah yes, excellent, excellent.'

We won that Test 20–14. With a foot injury ruling me out of the Tri-Nations series later in the year, that and Origin, which started a month later, were my only rep games for the season.

With the Broncos struggling, Wayne stood down as Origin coach and former Maroons halfback Mark Murray took over. Muppet was a bit like Wally in that he had been a player during the early days of Origin and had been known to be a bit of a party animal. Apparently one time he arrived at training in such a bad state that they had to put him on the wing, and even then he dropped so much ball that Artie Beetson called off training and they all headed off for lunch. But just like Wally, Muppet knew things had changed and he was a very serious coach. He was different from Wayne in that he was very intense. He liked to give a lot of instructions, but we still managed to have some laughs.

Early on in camp he got us together for a talk and was telling us how much Origin meant to players in the past. The new promotional poster was up on the wall behind him and he pointed to it and said, 'Look at this bloke here, Gary Larson.' He started telling us how much playing for Queensland had meant to Larso, and what a fearless competitor he had been. I couldn't have agreed with him more. When I was sitting at home watching the footy on TV as a 16-year-old, Gary Larson was one of my favourite players because of the way he would do 39 tackles a game and never give up. The only trouble was, the bloke on the poster wasn't Gary Larson. It was Darren Lockyer. There were four players on the poster – Locky, Steve Price, me and Shane Webcke – and they had superimposed our photos over a crowd scene. So when Muppet had stopped talking for a moment Wendell walked up to the poster and started looking very closely at the crowd scene. 'Oh yeah,' he says finally, 'here's Larso. He's eating a hot-dog in the crowd.'

Another time Muppet got us down in a room at our hotel to look at some game videos. I always reckon this is one of the funniest parts of camp, because no matter where you are, the coaches always have trouble working the VCR. Wayne is always trying to freeze-frame something and he hits the fast-forward, or if he tries to rewind he'll manage to turn the whole thing off. Whenever I read or hear about coaches doing some course to help them do their jobs, I think what they should be doing is a VCR technician's course. This day Muppet was pushing buttons and the video was going hay-wire. One second we had the NSW forwards running around in fast-forward, the next the TV was on and we were watching *Playschool*. Everyone in the team was suddenly a VCR expert. It's like, 'No Muppet, you've got to push the button with the squiggly line on it', 'That's it, Muppet, no, no. Push the rewind button, push the fast-forward.' Finally Muppet had to call the reception desk to get someone up to try to fix it. That's when we found out what had been going on. Muppet had the remote control for the TV instead of the one for the video. Wendell had grabbed the video remote when he walked into the room and was hiding it down under his seat. He'd been the one pushing the buttons while Muppet had been tearing his hair out.

But if we thought mucking around in camp was fun, it wasn't half as good as beating the Blues with a draw in the final match of the series. We got up 9–8 in the first game at Lang Park with Mat Rogers kicking a field goal, and in the second game, in Sydney, they scored a try after 42 seconds to win 12–8. The third was 10–all, although I thought I was going to score a try soon after half-time. I got the ball not far out and was heading for the line. I saw Laurie Daley coming across at me from one side and Spud Carroll coming from the other, but I thought I was going to beat them both to the line. Then Laurie tackled me and bang, I got belted from the other side. I remember thinking, 'Geez, Spud, that's a hard hit.' It turned out I'd hit the goalpost. I was lucky it had a lot of padding on it or they would have been taking me off on a stretcher.

It didn't matter, though. Ten–all was good enough for us to retain the trophy and we knew it. There was a lot of talk in the papers the next day about why we didn't go for a field goal, but I reckon the only people asking that question were from NSW. The same as in 2002. We knew the rules. We knew that because we held the shield we would keep it if the series was drawn. That was all we had set out to achieve, and if it drove the Blues crazy, all the better.

By the time Origin was over the Broncos had hit form. After Alfie had left we had close losses to Melbourne and the Roosters, games in which we had given everything. From there on we went 12 rounds without a loss. After the start we'd had it was like walking a tightrope every week. One slip and we were history. The game that really summed it up was our return match against the Roosters in Sydney.

It was a wet Friday night and we had some of the Denver Broncos as special guests in our dressing room. Denver has been our sister club since the Brisbane Broncos were formed in 1988, although you could say they are the rich sister. We went over there for our end of season trip in 1997 and they really looked after us. They took us right around their club and showed us their training facilities. It was unbelievable. To see match replays at the Broncos, we sit in a little room next to our training field at Gilbert Park with Wayne trying to work the video. They sit in a movie theatre. Everything was absolutely top of the line, and the king of Denver was their quarterback John Elway. When one of the Denver officials was driving us through town he was pointing left, right and centre saying, 'That's one of John's car yards, John has shares in that restaurant, that's John's bank.' Every second car on the road had a little strip around the numberplate saying John Elway 7, meaning it had been bought from one of his car yards. To show how well they looked after us, John Elway's father took us all out to dinner to a big steak restaurant at Winter Park, a ski resort. I remember there were all these skunks around outside and we all wanted to go out and look at them. The locals thought we were nuts, because skunks can squirt smelly stuff on you, but we wanted to see the Pepe Le Pews. Now I know how the Japanese tourists feel when they see a kangaroo or koala.

The biggest thrill was going to Mile High Stadium to see the Broncos play a game in front of 80,000 fans. They let us walk out on the centre of the ground with them for the warm-ups. It was pretty amazing. To pay them back, we let them come into a smelly muddy Sydney Football Stadium dressing room on a wet Friday night.

They were pretty impressed with the game, though. The thing they kept talking about was the fact that we played without helmets. Our fans were more interested in the fact that

Locky had kept our hopes alive with a field goal five seconds from the end. The Eels broke our winning streak the following week but a two-point win over Canterbury in the final round saw us beat Canberra into the last eight by just one point.

DAVID MIDDLETON Rugby League Yearbook 2000 *Players of the Year: During the Brisbane Broncos' incredible year of fluctuating fortunes, second-rower Gorden Tallis remained the single constant force. When the chips were down amid the worst start to a season in the club's 11 year history, Tallis was the one player who could hold his head high.*

He was Queensland's most effective forward during the State of Origin series, and a player around whom the selectors built their pack for Australia's Anzac Test team to play New Zealand.

The tangible rewards of Tallis' 1999 season were considerable. He was a resounding winner of the Broncos' Player of the Year title, he was Dally M second-rower of the year and his peers voted him the hardest player to tackle and the toughest competitor in an annual poll in Rugby League Week.

In every measure Tallis was the number one forward in rugby league in 1999, and he is expected to be among the first players selected at club, state and international level in season 2000.

We had gone from last place to the finals, and somehow, even after that shocking start to the year and losing Alf, we made it to the major semi-final against Cronulla. They were a hot side that year – they probably should have gone all the way to the Grand Final. We certainly didn't give them much opposition. It was one of those days for us. Andrew Gee got knocked out in the first 30 seconds and we never came back. Towards the end of the game Mat Rogers ran 20 metres for a try, showing us the ball all the way. After that, when we were standing behind the try-line waiting for the conversion, someone in the crowd started playing 'The Last Post' on a bugle.

That said it all. I didn't know whether to laugh or cry.

CHAPTER TEN

2000

We won it at Canungra. I know that Jack Gibson used to say that 'winning starts on Monday', but for us in 2000 it started a month before the first game, when we got on a bus and headed south towards Beaudesert. Canungra army base is about 50 km from Brisbane and we were all pretty relaxed on the trip playing cards, eating muesli bars and lollies and having a laugh. If we'd known what was waiting for us we'd probably never have got on board. Most of us had been to Canungra for pre-season training before. It is always tough: a day of obstacle courses, marches with full backpacks. We'd climb some ropes, get a bit muddy, that sort of thing, but after the disappointment of 1999, Canungra 2000 was different. I don't know who dreamed it up, but whoever it was has a very twisted mind.

The bus stopped about 10 km out from camp and an army trainer climbed in and told us to put on some comfortable joggers. He said we were going to 'march in'. His idea of marching was obviously different from mine. We ran the whole way, stopping just long enough to pick up some long, heavy ropes which took six blokes to carry. We'd gone six kilometres when Lote Tuqiri fainted. I'm not saying he was faking it, but I've always thought it was interesting that after running all that way on rough roads Lote collapsed on soft grass under a shady tree. When we went back before the 2003 season we were going to put a cross on the spot in remembrance of our fallen comrade.

When we got to the camp, the army blokes let us have a swim in the pool to cool off – and made us tread water for 10 minutes. From there we went straight to the obstacle course. By the time we finished that, it was dinner, during which they gave us a course in orienteering and map reading. I remember there were plenty of jokes that night. We thought we'd done pretty well. It had been tough but we'd got through it, and when we bedded down in tents that night we thought we'd be back on the bus the next day.

We woke up at 3 am to the sound of machine-gun fire. Some lunatic was standing outside our tent shooting blanks and screaming at us to get up. They gave us 10 minutes to get dressed and strap on 30 kg backpacks and webbings. They split us up into three groups of eight and got us started climbing up a steep hill. And climbing and climbing and climbing.

As we went up that hill we had to pick up more of those

ropes, ammunition boxes filled with old bullet shells and metre-long steel rods. We each had to carry a jerry can filled with water plus the group had a big 20-litre water drum which had to be brought along as well. Shane Webcke picked up the water drum when we headed off and didn't let anyone else carry it for the whole first session. He decided it was his responsibility and he wasn't going to back down no matter how hard it got. We climbed for four hours before they finally called a halt and gave us half an hour for breakfast. Then we started walking – and we walked all day.

There was more to it than that, though: there were activities along the way. Sometimes we would walk, then run, then walk again. Other times we would be given a task, like pushing a trailer up the hill for three kilometres. It was one of those big army trailers which would have been hard enough to push if it was in mint condition, but this one was missing a wheel. They gave us a log and a length of rope and we had to work out how to make the thing work. One time we had to get another trailer across a weir. This one had all its wheels but that didn't help us too much. We got it halfway across and the thing sank straight to the bottom. So we had to get it out again, and all the time we were under the stopwatch, with each group earning points for how fast and how well they did things. We had to climb down a gorge and cross a river on ropes, with our backpacks on, before heading up the other side. That task had a built-in challenge. If you didn't stay dry getting across the river, going up the gorge would have been torture. At one stage one of the army trainers pointed at me and said, 'This man has a broken leg, get him to the next checkpoint', so the rest of the boys had to make a stretcher and carry me for about three kilometres.

It was like that the whole way. We were pushed until we were almost exhausted, then given some information that placed us in a certain situation. We had to weigh up our options, work out a solution and put it into practice. And push on. For one of the tasks we came to a clearing and there were 15 items – another one of those ropes, three ammo boxes, a heap of big tyres. We had 20 minutes to get them up a hill. That's eight blokes, 15 items, just under seven minutes a trip, some blokes capable of carrying more than others. Try figuring that out when you've been dragging yourself through the bush since 3 am.

It was interesting watching the way people reacted. Some really struggled in some areas, some in others. Like I said, Webbie really got into it, he took it as a personal challenge. Darren Lockyer was exactly as you would expect – he just cruised through, the way he always does. Petero Civoniceva was cramping by 9 am and finished with giant blisters on his feet, but he just never gave up. Others just couldn't cop some part of the course – maybe the rope or the trailer. With me it was this 20-litre water container. I was buggered – we all were – but I was going okay. I struggled in some things but managed others. And then it was my turn to carry the group water drum. I tried everything I could think of: taking everything out of my backpack and trying to push the drum in there, putting a rope around it and dragging it. Nothing worked. Nothing. It broke me. I was nearly crying.

Looking back on it now, I know I was looking for an easy way. I thought there must be a short cut, but there wasn't. Finally I just had to wrap my arms around the bloody thing and carry it up that hill. I don't think I've ever felt more stuffed in my life. I wasn't the only one either. Mick Hancock had to do the same thing in one of the other groups. Wayne reckoned that he was standing at the top of the hill when Mick got up there with the container in his arms – and Wayne moved away because he saw Mick's eyes and he was fair dinkum scared that Mick might kill him.

We went until 4 pm. I remember getting to a clearing and there waiting for us was an apple, a Mars bar and a bottle of Coke – and it was the best apple, Mars bar and Coke I've ever had in my life. That night when we crawled back into our sleeping bags, each of the groups was treated differently. One got two ration packs to share between eight blokes, but when they bedded down, no sleep. Another group got no food, but they were left alone all night. The message was, you had to give up something, food or sleep. You couldn't have both. My group climbed in to bed at 6 pm, still wearing our backpacks. The machine guns started at 10 pm, then every two hours all night. By 4 am I couldn't give a rat's where that bloke with the machine-gun was, I just wanted some sleep.

By the time we climbed back on that bus the next afternoon we had marched about 40 km, carrying out different tasks under extreme pressure. The biggest buzz we got was when Steve, the bloke in charge, told us, 'When you walked through the gates on day one, you blokes looked like footballers. When you came out the bush after finishing the course you looked like soldiers. You looked like a team.'

I honestly believe that was when we won the 2000 premiership. After that, no-one was going to beat us. Obviously it didn't make us better footballers. It wasn't going to make us run over a bloke or tackle harder, but it made us tougher mentally. It started on the training paddock. In the past we

171

might have thought a 90-minute training session was tough, but after pushing a one-wheeled trailer up a hill for 45 minutes we realised maybe it wasn't so tough after all. Like with me and the container of water, it showed us that there is no easy way, and that sometimes all you can do is just keep going. And after going through the bush for 14 or 15 hours straight, the 80 minutes it takes to play a football game didn't seem all that long. I'm not saying we ever thought about it consciously; we never said something like, 'I've lived through Canungra, I can do this', but it was there. We'd done it, and it moved the barriers in our minds. What we had thought was the limit of our endurance before was now further down the track.

I reckon it showed from the very first game of the competition. We came away from Campbelltown Showground with a 24–all draw, but to me that draw was as good as a win. That was the Wests Tigers first ever game, and Balmain's greatest supporter, Laurie Nichols, had died just days before. If ever the Tigers were going to win one, this was it. To make matters worse, the ground wasn't ready – it was covered in sand. It was like playing on the beach.

The next week Kevvie was out and I captained the Broncos for the first time – in a Friday night game against Brian Smith's Parramatta side, as it happened. Actually it was the first time I had captained a side since the Under 18s in Townsville. Captaincy wasn't anything I had ever really thought about. I was just the young bloke at Saints, and Alfie and Kevvie had always been in charge at the Broncos, but when Alfie retired Wayne had taken me aside and told me he was making me vice-captain. I couldn't tell you his thinking – maybe he thought it would make me more responsible –

but I do know that captaincy has been good for me. I've always felt that the captain doesn't necessarily have to be the best player in the team. He has to be the player who reacts to having the captaincy the best. If you look at the Broncos it's obvious to me that Darren Lockyer is our best player, but I don't know if having the (c) next to his name would make Locky play any better than he does. Maybe Wayne thought that if I was captain I would react harder and play better. Maybe he thought the other players would react well to me.

WAYNE BENNETT: I made him captain for two reasons. One, he needed to challenge himself more or he'd go to sleep, and two, because he is inspirational. All our captains have been inspirational. We don't have a captain who doesn't lead from the front. We don't need someone to talk; I do enough talking for 10 captains. We need someone to do what has to be done on the field. When Gorden is full of emotion he can't give a speech, but gee he can put on a great hit or go for a big run. That's why he's captain.

Before the Parramatta game Kevvie gave me a lot of help. Actually, he might have given me too much help. To try something different, we had stayed down in Sydney after the Tigers match and gone into camp at a hotel in Bondi. Our new media manager, Tony Durkin, had organised a meet-the-media barbecue lunch on the roof garden on the Monday, and

Kevvie and I sat down for a quiet beer when they left. We were still up there having a quiet one when it was time to go out to dinner. I do remember one thing he said, though: 'If you want to win, you have to be the one who leads the way.' It was good advice and I took it to heart. The day of the game I was feeling great. I reckon it's only happened to me about three times in my life, but I knew I was going to have a big one and that the team was going to go well. Another time it happened was before the first Origin in 2001, the one where Wayne came back to coach and we had all the young blokes. Wayne was pretty nervous the day before the game but I just knew everything was going to be okay. I said to him, 'Coach, don't worry. We're going to win tomorrow', and we did. It was the same that day in Sydney. It's hard to explain, but I had a real warm feeling. A mate of mine rang up to wish me luck and asked how I thought I'd go. I've never done this before or since, but I said to him, 'If you want to make some money, put a bet on me winning man of the match.' I don't know if he did, but he would have collected.

From there on there was no stopping us. When we went nine rounds without a loss the media was asking, 'Who will the Broncos be playing in the Grand Final?' We never thought about it like that. We kept our minds on the job, but it was a pretty outstanding year. We lost six games all year and, with no disrespect to the blokes who had to fill in, four of them were when eight of us were playing Origin.

I'd like to say the Origin series was as successful for us as the premiership, but it wasn't. It was the one where I had my big run-in with Bill Harrigan. I'll go into all that in depth in the next chapter, but let's just say that Bill had a major influence on the series that year. We had game one in Sydney in our grasp when he missed two knock-ons that led to the Blues tying up the game. Then he sent me off and they scored again to go one game up. Trailing after the first game changes the entire build-up to game two. You need to throw everything at the opposition to square the series, but at the same time, if you try something that doesn't work, you risk losing the series. Bill reckoned he needed a police escort for game two in Brisbane after the roasting he got on radio talk-back, but apart from some boos from the crowd he was never in any danger. The same could be said for the Blues. They took the game and the series, and the media jumped on me for saying that we shouldn't even show up for game three back in Sydney. Judging by the result, you'd think we didn't. They won 56–16 in one of the most depressing nights of my career.

That business of me saying we shouldn't play the dead rubber was typical of the way things I say get blown up in the media. What happened was, immediately after the second game as I sat in the dressing room feeling as if I wanted to jump off a bridge, a reporter came to me and asked whether I thought we should have to play the third game. I said something like, 'Well, when you consider what they do in the US baseball and basketball, maybe the league should think about it. Over there these multi-million dollar businesses hold best-of series and if one team gets into a position where they can't lose they don't have to play the rest. Rugby league is a million dollar industry too. It's something they could look at.' When the papers came out the next day they didn't say anything about US baseball or basketball, just that Gorden Tallis reckoned we shouldn't play game three. I'm not blue-ing about it, just pointing out the way it happened.

In 2002 I wrote a weekly newspaper column for the *Courier-Mail* and that taught me a lot about the way the media works. You can have all these opinions about things, but you have to say them in a way that makes sure people won't stop reading after the first paragraph. You have to pull out the controversial stuff and put it up the top. I understand that, but sometimes it can cause problems, especially for someone like me who likes to say things. When a reporter asks me for my opinion, I'll tell them. I couldn't be one of those people who just says whatever they think won't get them into strife. I try to be honest, but at the same time I like journalists to be honest with me. Usually they are, but sometimes I've been burnt. I guess it gets down to treating people the way you'd want them to treat you. Not long ago I was at a function with a reporter who hasn't always been straight with me. He was so drunk that the bar staff refused to serve him, but his mates kept getting him beers. Then the security guard came up and asked him to leave. The security bloke was very friendly, very laid-back, but the journo got aggressive. I was only drinking light beer, and managed to settle everyone down. The journo said he would leave when he had finished his beer, but a little while later I looked over and there he was with a full glass. I said to him, 'Funny isn't it? If I was carrying on like you are it would be in your column tomorrow, but we won't be reading about your behaviour, will we?' He said, 'No, no, you're wrong. If I heard something about you I'd ring you and get your side of things.' Somehow I didn't believe him. Still, dealing with the media is just part of the game, and for the most part I've learnt to cop it and move on.

Thinking about it now, I wish we hadn't played that third Origin game in 2000. The Blues were on fire, and even though we wanted to put on a good show, we didn't have it in us. It was the five per cent theory that I spoke about before, where a team just five per cent off its maximum game can lose by 20 or 30 points, except on this night we were probably down 7 or 8 per cent and they were close to 100. I remember the last meeting we had before the game, when Mat Rogers got up and told us how hard he was going to play. I never like to say too much before a game. I just like to go out and play. There's always the risk of your words coming back to bite you on the bum. Unfortunately for Matty, that's what happened that night. He'd told us that he was going to give it everything he had. He was going to charge into the forwards, tackle everything in blue, play out of his skin. 'I'm going to try so hard you'll have to carry me off the field,' he said. Well, after they'd put over 50 points on us, Wendell and I thought we'd better help Mat live up to his words. As soon as we got into the dressing room we picked him up, carried him into the showers and threw him in. That was the one light moment of the night. Humiliated, embarrassed, guilty . . . use whatever word you want. I don't think I've ever felt lower.

Still, at least we were still on track at the Broncos. Week after week we were grinding down the opposition with a style which was a bit of a departure from our old razzle-dazzle. With the loss of Alfie, we changed the way we played. We became more structured, relying more on the slow build-up and less on individual brilliance. That's not to say that we hadn't had any structure in the past. Every team has to have that; if you just work off the top of your head you'll have nothing to fall back on. But during the Alfie years, when we got a roll on, Alfie would go to the line and nine times out of ten hit the right person with a pass. Without him there, we relied more on our forward pack to provide go forward. I'd say if you looked at the stats for the year you'd see that a lot of our games were pretty close at half-time, but that with about 20 minutes to go we'd blow the opposition away. We even did it in the qualifying final against the Sharks at ANZ. We were down 20–6 at half-time but came back to win 34–20. Nobody was saying anything about Canungra that afternoon, but I reckon it was there.

It was the same with our defence. Like the Roosters in 2002, a lot of our wins were set up by our defence. Even though that year there were a lot of rule changes aimed at helping the attacking side, in the 25 games that all of us played, only three teams scored more than 20 points against us. Compare that with the Bulldogs, a team known for its defence, who had 20 points scored against them 13 times. Attack wins crowds, but defence wins premierships.

DAVID MIDDLETON, Rugby League Yearbook 2001 *Team of the Year: Gorden Tallis could never be accused of lacking passion. Everything the big Queenslander does comes straight from the heart. And while that can have its drawbacks, it's a quality that takes him where he wants to go more often than not.*

It is almost a formality that he will ascend to the Queensland captaincy in 2001. He will succeed Kevin Walters as captain of the Broncos and after being named vice-captain of Australia's World Cup side, the national captaincy would also appear to await him.

Brisbane coach Wayne Bennett, who will take charge of the

Maroons in 2001, offered this insight into Tallis' personality: 'He pulls no punches. That's the integrity of the guy. He's all character. There's no grey areas with Gorden. Not in the matter of character and his value system. There's no negotiation.'

Tallis wins friends with his disarming honesty. He wins the respect of footballers with pure talent.

Once again he dominated Rugby League Week's *annual players' poll. He was rated the hardest hitter, the hardest player to tackle and the man most players did not want to pick a fight with.*

He earns respect, he provides inspiration, and above everything else, he has passion. What more could a captain want?

When we made it to the Grand Final to play the Roosters, a lot of people thought there was a sense of inevitability about it. I know a mate of mine went to the game and was standing with some Roosters fans. They told him, 'We're not going to win, but we're so happy to be here.'

I suppose as a spectacle it wasn't the best. We won 14–6, and if anyone watching was disappointed, I can assure you that none of the Broncos players or staff were. That game was one of the most emotional I've ever been involved in. We didn't stand around beforehand and say, 'Let's do it for Kevvie', but it was hard to escape. Every reporter who asked a question or wrote a story made the point that the little bloke was playing his last game for the club after 11 seasons. Of course he came back when the club needed him the next year, but we weren't to know that. Add in the fact that Mick Hancock, the last of the Broncos to have played in the first game in 1988, was retiring after the match and that Brad Thorn, Kevin Campion and Tonie Carroll were heading elsewhere and there was plenty of feeling around the club when we brought back the trophy.

As Wayne Bennett said, 'I've never seen so many blokes with tears in their eyes after a game.'

We celebrated long and hard that night. Some of us went right through from the time we got back to the club after flying back from Sydney to the next night. Others went home for a quick shower and a nap and joined up again. Wayne was one of those. He doesn't drink, never has, but he was with us all the way until he dropped out, went home for a shower and changed and came back to the club. By late that night we were down on the oval where we train, sitting in front of a giant bonfire. It was the inner circle only. We had celebrated with our supporters at the club, posed for the press photographs and waved at the TV cameras, but now it was our time. We'd come a long way since we'd climbed off that bus at Canungra, and we had achieved everything we had set out to do. One by one, as we went around the circle, we climbed to our feet and said a few words about the team and what it had meant to us. Some of us didn't make a lot of sense. Others – particularly the blokes who were leaving – said some amazing things. I can't remember the exact words, but I'll never forget the feelings they brought. And then it was Wayne's turn. The bloke who had never had a drink in his life climbed to his feet, picked up a stubbie, raised it to us in salute and took a little sip. Then he sat down again.

Sometimes Wayne doesn't have to say a word to say a hell of a lot.

CHAPTER ELEVEN

HOLLYWOOD
BILL

I couldn't believe he didn't see them. Two knock-ons that cost us the Origin series and gave me a reputation which I'll probably never shake. It was Origin I, 2000. We were on top in a typically tough match, with the Blues throwing everything at us. First David Furner spilled it, then Terry Hill. And Bill Harrigan missed them both.

That's when I started giving it to him.

'You're kidding, Bill, what about the knock-ons?' As the game continued, I didn't give up. Following the play, moving up in defence, I just kept yelling. 'Enjoy it while you can, Bill. Stephen Clark will be ref for the next game. See ya, Bill, you're reffing your last Origin. You've really blown it now, Bill. That was a big mistake, how could you miss it? Stephen Clark will be in now for sure.'

I know it sounds childish, but I was furious. It is just so important to win the first match of the series. In almost 70 Origin matches, only about three or four teams who have lost the first match go on to win the series. Everything hinges on it. If you win that first game you go into the second match with nothing to lose. You can throw everything you have at it because even if you lose you can still take the series in the third game. Lose the first match and you are on a tightrope. Much as you need to risk everything to take game two, you still know that if something doesn't come off and you lose, that's it for the year. Thanks for coming.

So when Harrigan missed those knock-ons and called 'play-on' I was spitting chips. And when Ryan Girdler scored later in that set of six, I went right off. Adrian Lam was captain and I was vice-captain. We both got to Bill at the same time. I was screaming at him, pleading with him to go to the video ref for a ruling on the knock-ons. I didn't know if he could, all I knew was that he had missed two blatant infringements and it had cost us four points, tying it up 16–all and bringing the Blues back into the game. I reckon 60,000 at the game and millions watching on TV had all seen what had happened. Everyone in the country except Bill Harrigan. Everyone in our team had eased off a bit when Furner and Hill knocked-on, expecting Bill to blow the whistle. The Blues had, too. When he didn't, they couldn't believe their luck.

I have to admit, I was seeing red when I charged up to Bill, pointing back to where the knock-ons had happened and making the square with my hands, the signal for the video ref. He ignored me, pointed at the spot to signal the try and blew his whistle.

'Bill,' I pleaded, 'please, have another look. There were two knock-ons. Please, go to the video.'

He told me to get away.

'Go over there,' he said gesturing behind the posts. 'I've made my decision.'

I didn't move, I was just so furious.

That's when I said it.

'Mate, you're a f——ing cheat.'

'What did you say?'

'You heard me. There are 17 blokes out here trying their guts out for Queensland and you're going to ruin it with a poor decision like that.'

'Be quiet. I've had enough of you. I've made my decision, I can't go to the screen.'

'Well you're a f——ing cheat.'

'If you call me a cheat one more time I'm going to send you off.'

I stared into his eyes and said: 'You haven't got the balls to send me off.'

Guess what? He did have the balls.

As I walked off, with the Sydney crowd going berserk, the Channel 9 camera was stuck in my face. I looked behind it and saw Joe the Cameraman, the bloke who had been at the centre of the 'can't throw, can't bowl' drama. I was in no mood to be friendly.

'Get that camera out of my face,' I said. He kept filming me. 'Get that f——ing camera out of my face,' I said again. He did.

I can't really remember what happened when I walked into the dressing room. I was too upset. All I know is that from that moment on I've been remembered for the spray I gave Bill Harrigan and the so-called problems I have with referees. One of the best things I ever did was tackle Brett Hodgson and drag him over the sideline in the 2002 series so that the TV stations had some new Origin footage of me to use. Up until then it was always of me screaming at Bill and getting sent off.

After the game, which we lost 20–16 after playing one man short for the last nine minutes, I went to the referees' room to apologise. I said, 'Mate, I'm sorry I said that.' Bill, as always needing to get the last word in, said, 'That's okay. Let's not let it happen again.' Then I waited around for the judiciary hearing, which was held at the ground. The judiciary ruled that the sending off had been penalty enough and I went out to face the media. By then I was feeling pretty bad about what had happened. Not so much that I had questioned the ruling, because as vice-captain I was within my rights to do that, but because of the way I had done it and the way I had spoken to Bill in front of millions of people watching on TV. I knew I had set a bad example to young players and kids around the country and I wanted to say so. I told the media that I had been wrong to blow up like that and that it had cost my team the match. I said, 'Bill Harrigan doesn't tell me how to play, I shouldn't have tried to tell him how to referee.' But if I thought that was going to be the end of it, I was sadly mistaken. For days it seemed no-one could talk about anything else. Bill had told the press immediately after the game that he didn't think he had made any mistakes and that he had got the decision on that try 100 per cent right. Talkback radio and Letters to the Editor in the Queensland papers were full of it. Everyone had an opinion, even the Queensland premier, Peter Beattie.

COURIER-MAIL – Letters to the Editor, June 2000:

Again, the actions of referee Bill Harrigan cost Queensland a State of Origin game. We were in it until he blew time-on.

DS, Burleigh.

Bill Harrigan has turned me off a series of football matches that I have watched with great joy for years. I will never watch another State of Origin or NRL match.

MH, Tamworth, NSW.

At least no-one can ever again accuse State of Origin rugby league referee Bill Harrigan of being biased toward Queensland or the Broncos.

DM, Imbil.

If Gorden Tallis played AFL, he could have rendered the referee unconscious and got on with the game. There isn't a penalty in AFL for that, is there?

JC, Kenmore.

From what I have observed, the height of hypocrisy is a footballer of any code calling a referee a cheat.

GA, Kenmore Hills.

I watched the State of Origin game on TV and, of course, saw the knock-ons. I've watched it again on tape (twice) and have to admit a send-off was absolutely essential. Harrigan should have gone.

FHQ, Main Beach.

Premier Peter Beattie confirms he is a media tart and pleads to be referee for the second State of Origin rugby league match. How high does he want his career to take him? Official parachute tester?

TS, Mt Nebo.

What a great contest we witnessed in the first State of Origin rugby league match. It's a shame the game was marred by such a poor performance by referee Bill Harrigan and the seemingly nonexistent linesmen. I hope ARL officials review the video of the game. It will reveal at least nine forward passes, involving both teams, went unpunished. One can understand Harrigan missing forward passes from dummy half when he is standing back behind the defensive line, but surely this is why we have linesmen. While Harrigan's decision to remove Gorden Tallis must be supported, we should take into account the frustration caused by Harrigan's failure to call a very obvious knock-on by New South Wales, particularly when this decision, or lack of decision, led to the winning try by New South Wales.

MS, Banksia Beach.

Advice for Queenslanders: get over it. No amount of whingeing is going to change the decision. Accept defeat graciously and hope that, in two weeks, your boys can prove that they deserved to win. The scoreboard says 1–0 in favour of New South Wales, like it or not. Advice for Gorden Tallis: shut your mouth and let your ability do the talking. I hope I have helped you all deal with it.

PD, Eatons Hill.

How many times has Gorden Tallis seen a referee or umpire change his ruling because a player has told him, in very strong terms that he made a mistake? How many times has a player been sent off for telling the referee off? I have never reached the heights that Tallis has but I learnt early that, even if he is wrong, the man in white is always right. Tallis played well until he was sent off but he left us a man short when it counted. The most humble player knows that you cannot change a referee's mind. Why doesn't Tallis?

NG, Kingston.

I have sympathy for Gorden Tallis. I know referee Harrigan has a very difficult job to do but he did not use the video referee to his full potential, consequently missing forward passes, knock-ons and 'hands in play'. These all gave NSW the benefit on the night. Tallis is a dedicated team player. I commend his persistence in promoting fair play and do not think he should feel the burden of Queensland's loss on his shoulders.

NB, Carbrook.

Bill Harrigan's refereeing was the worst in 20 years of Origin football. The late high hits, the knock-ons and stealing of the ball in tackles by NSW without penalty were enough to upset anyone.

GLJ, Gladstone.

No fair-minded rugby league follower would deny Queensland deserved to win the first State of Origin. However, we witness bad decisions in every game. Gorden Tallis carried on like a spoilt child and left Bill Harrigan with no choice but to march him. Your headline 'Woeful Harrigan Robs Maroons' says it all. Perhaps the catch cry for this state should be 'great winners one day, whingeing losers the next'.

FE, Wishart.

My phone was still ringing off the hook with media wanting to get me to blow up again. Finally I just stopped answering my mobile altogether if I didn't recognise the number on the screen.

Two days after the game, the mobile was ringing and I recognised the number of Broncos chief executive Shane Edwards. He told me that Bill Harrigan had been trying to contact me but I hadn't picked up.

'He's going to ring as soon as I hang up,' he said. 'It's a Sydney number, so make sure you take the call.'

The crazy thing was that up until that game I had always got along well with Bill. I like to have a friendly, joking relationship with people, and that's how it had been with Bill and me since I had gone over to New Zealand for Gary Freeman's testimonial match. It was one of those light-hearted matches where old players take part alongside some of the current players. There were blokes like Mark Graham, Brent Todd, Clayton Friend, Benny Elias, Garry Jack, Brett Kenny, Blocker Roach and Royce Simmons and some newer blokes like me. We were over there for three days to play the game, attend a big dinner and generally have a good time and Bill was brought over to referee. We all played golf and had a few drinks together and Bill and I hit it off pretty well. By the end of the trip I was calling him by his nicknames – Hollywood or Bill Arrogant – and he was calling me by mine, Kettle. After that, whenever we played a game that he was refereeing we'd nod or have a bit of a joke and I'd always make sure I thanked him afterwards. So when the Sydney call came through on my mobile I had no worries taking it.

'Gorden,' he said, 'just about the other night. I wanted to clear the air. I've had a look at the tape and there were two knock-ons. You had the right to question them. I didn't see them, and I didn't get a call from my linesmen.'

That was fine with me. We're all human. Players make mistakes and so do referees – but I still didn't think that in the pressure cooker of Origin I deserved to get marched. I said to him, 'Bill, how could you send me off? I call you a cheat every time you referee me.' He laughed and said, 'Mate, I didn't send you off because you called me a cheat. I sent you off because for the four tackles before that you'd been saying Stephen Clark was a better referee than me.'

After that, things went back to normal as far as we were concerned. We would still have a laugh and a joke before, after and even during a game, like I do with all the refs – not that anyone would believe it. The media was still going on about what had happened in the Origin match, and every time Bill was in charge of a Broncos game there would be some mention in the press of the 'Tallis–Harrigan feud'. As far as I was concerned, there was no problem at all. Right up until 2002, that is.

The turning point came in game one of the series in Sydney. The Blues were up by about 15 points late in the first half and Bill was really giving it to us in the penalty count. At one stage before half-time he gave NSW four penalties in a row, mostly against Alfie, who had made a second comeback to the Broncos and Origin that season, for not getting back onside. The thing with Alfie was that he was very rarely onside throughout his whole career. It was a bit of joke at the Broncos that all you would hear on the field was the referee saying, 'Come on Alf, get back onside.' So when Bill called me out as captain that night I couldn't help but make a joke. He told me to get Alfie back onside or he would have to take some action. He said, 'I'm sick of giving these penalties.' I said, 'Bill, fair go, he's 39 years old, look at how fat he is. How can you expect him to keep onside?'

He didn't laugh; he just waved me away. I suppose I should have taken the tip.

It is a well-known fact that Bill doesn't like blowing the whistle. He likes to keep the game flowing. But I still stand by the fact that he never said he would send off the next bloke who infringed. If he had, I would have said something to the players, but I didn't. I just ran back into position and got on with the game. Soon afterwards I tackled Jason Moodie on the halfway. He lashed out with his boot and I gave him a shove. I didn't think it was bad enough for a penalty, and it didn't slow the game down, but Bill obviously thought differently. He blew the whistle and held up ten fingers. I looked at him in shock and he said, 'I told you the next player who infringed would be sent to the sin-bin.' Well, maybe it was like school all over again, and I hadn't listened, but I still reckon he never said it.

I didn't say a word to him; I just turned and walked off. When I saw a replay of the game on video, I saw Bill walking off at half-time with Alfie, Andrew Gee and Kevin Campion walking behind him, giving him a gobfull. These were blokes with 600 games under their belts, so I guess I wasn't the only one who found it strange. By the time I got back on, the game was well and truly lost, and my relationship with Bill Harrigan had hit rock bottom. I never said anything to him about it; I guess we both said what we wanted to say to the media that night. He said he told me the next man who infringed would be off, I said he didn't, and that was that.

As had happened two years earlier, it was the media that really kept the thing bubbling along. It got to the stage where I got sick of going to media conferences after games because all anyone wanted to ask me about was how I got along with the referee. Finally I said to the press after one game, 'Next time I come in here, if you blokes don't ask me about the game and how I played or how the team played, I won't be coming again.' Not that it seemed to put them off. As far as they were concerned, the Tallis–Harrigan feud was back on in earnest, and while there had never really been a feud, I started thinking a lot about my relationship, not just with Bill, but with all referees in general. It didn't help that two and a half weeks later I had that blow up with Brian Smith after his players said they had been sent out to tell the referee I had been bad-mouthing him. That started me worrying that I could be a liability to the team, someone who could be exploited by the opposition. If that was the case, I might have a problem as captain.

I went to Wayne and asked him, 'Do I have a problem?' He told me he didn't think so, but he was still prepared to take some action. I think all coaches are in contact with the referees' bosses, and one day at training Wayne came up and told me that Peter Louis and Graham Annersley were in town. He said, 'Mate, the refs' coaches are up here to have a talk to me today. You should come along, clear up a few things.'

It was very interesting meeting – it was good to see things from another side. At the time I was down on referees. I was thinking, what do I have to do to get a fair deal? Peter Louis told me the referees were thinking, what can we do to shut Gorden Tallis up? Peter told me the referees found me very intimidating. My comeback to that was that I am a physical player, I lead my troops in a physical way, by showing them what I am prepared to do to win the game. Peter said that was fine, but I should try to speak to them clearly and quietly. It was a good meeting and I think we made some headway, but if the referees were waiting for me to take my mouthguard out and talk with a plum in my mouth, well sorry, that was not going to happen.

In saying that, I do think the referees do a great job, and it's not easy, especially since they've been wired for sound. Having seen up close what they go through, you'll never get me doing the job when my playing days are over. They can have it all to themselves.

After word of my meeting with Peter Louis and Graham

Annersley got out, the media starting wondering if Bill Harrigan and I would have a meeting to clear the air. The Broncos' media man, Tony Durkin, was talking to the NRL's media guy John Brady about trying to set something up. Durko was getting calls from the press every day, and he asked me what he should say. My initial reaction was, 'No, I'm not talking to him, why should I?', but after thinking about it for a while I thought, 'Why not, what harm can it do?' I told Durko to keep it quiet from the media but to try to organise it. He arranged for us to meet down in Sydney before our game against the Bulldogs at the Showground.

We needed a venue where we wouldn't be spotted, so Bill suggested his parents' home. I got a cab from our hotel at Coogee and Bill was waiting on the front lawn when I got there. He took me inside and introduced me to his parents, who are just lovely people. It was funny to see Bill, who is so in charge and strict on the field, being the nice, polite, respectful son. His father was a real rugby league supporter. I think he might have been a St George fan. I asked him, 'Can't you keep your son under control?' Bill's mum offered me a cup of tea and some biscuits but I just had some water. I think Young William might have had a cuppa and some bickies. We had what they call 'honest dialogue'.

I said to him, 'What's wrong with the way I captain the side?' He said, 'In the past you used to talk to me in a productive way. We could be honest with each other. That's not happening out there now.' I have to give him credit, he didn't hold back. He said, 'I think you're struggling as a player. You're frustrated out there and looking for an easy way out.'

He probably had me there; I was getting frustrated because I was coming back from major injury and I didn't think I was playing as well as I would have liked. I told him he was making sense, but that didn't stop me giving it straight back to him.

'What about you?' I said. 'In the past, players used to give you a hard time and it was like water off a duck's back. Now it worries you.'

'Maybe I am a bit like an old player,' he said. 'I know there's a push for Paul Simpkins to get the Grand Final. I'm feeling it a bit.'

The true confessions out of the way, we got down to business. He gave me some good tips. He said as captain it was up to me to help keep the game flowing. He said if I wanted to say something or question a decision, I should wait for a break of play. I see his point. I wouldn't want to be a Geoff Toovey, running up and questioning the ref about every play, but at the same time, in a game of rugby league something can happen and there won't be a break in play for three or four minutes. Let's just say I took on board what he said, and I hope he took on board what I said. When we finished he drove me back to Coogee and dropped me a block from the hotel so I could sneak back in without anyone seeing. By the time I got out of the car we were laughing, like old times, and it's been like that ever since.

The test came in the elimination final against the Roosters. I walked up to him a couple of times to question decisions and he gave me a straight answer without any problems. Then in the 65th minute he penalised us for being offside. I was going to blow up. I said 'Bill . . .'

He said, 'Mate, they weren't onside.'

'What about them?' I said, gesturing towards the Roosters. 'They've been offside for 10 weeks.'

He said, 'I wasn't refereeing those games.'

And that was it. No drama, no headlines – much as the media would have loved it.

It's no scoop that Bill and I have had our problems, but he is still the best referee I have ever played under. The thing I like about him is that he can admit when he is wrong. He came out publicly and said he was wrong to send me to the sin-bin in that Origin game. It was a bit late, but I accepted it, and it takes a man to admit his mistakes. Sometimes he must have wondered whether it was worth it. He said he was wrong that time and nothing happened, but after that game in which he sent four Parramatta players to the sin-bin against Newcastle he came out and said he was right – and got dropped to reserve grade for a week.

Still, as far as I'm concerned, my problems with Bill are old news; the more they are dragged up, the more chance there is of someone trying to exploit them the way Parramatta did that day. I've been asked about him so many times that one day I just decided, that's it, I'm not answering any more questions about him. He must be just as sick of hearing my name as I am of hearing his. All I know is that I am fine with Bill Harrigan. I don't have a problem with him and I don't think he has a problem with me.

But I still can't believe he missed those two knock-ons.

CHAPTER TWELVE

ON TOP OF
THE WORLD

It started out looking as if it would be one of my best ever seasons. Then at one stage it looked like being my last.

Everything had been going so well. We had the 2000 premiership trophy safely locked away at the club, in the off-season I'd been Australian vice-captain when we won the World Cup and then Wayne gave me the Broncos captaincy. And if all that wasn't enough, the first match of the 2001 Origin series gave me one of the best nights of my life. It's just as well we can't see what's around the corner. Sometimes it'd give you nightmares.

For me the 2000 season never really ended. It was as if we

went straight from the Grand Final into training for the World Cup and from there we went straight into the 2001 season. Not that I was complaining. Everything just seemed to get better and better.

The World Cup campaign started off with a warm-up match against Papua New Guinea in Townsville. I always love playing in Townsville. For me it's going home, and to play a Test match there for my country, whether it's against England, New Zealand or PNG, is a huge thrill – not just for me, but for my whole family. There are always a lot of distractions for me when I play in Townsville. I get together with friends and family and generally have a pretty good time. My preparation there is a lot different from my preparation for other matches, but this year we were there for a week before the game so I was able to get all the distractions out of the way early.

I know some people don't think the Tests against PNG are too tough, mainly because of the size of the scorelines and the size of the Kumuls, but I can tell you, honestly, they are pretty hard games. As a forward, the games are a lottery. I reckon you get more bumps and bruises against the Kumuls than in any other game. The PNG players don't have any thoughts about safety and they don't always have the right technique in the tackle, which means someone is going to get hurt. You only have to go over there and see how many players end up in wheelchairs after spear-tackles. The first year Brisbane Lions coach Leigh Matthews organised the all-codes charity lunch in Brisbane, Wayne decided to donate our share of the money to spinal care in PNG. They love their footy, though. It is the only country in the world where rugby league is the national sport – they idolise anyone who

197

plays in the NRL. I reckon when we go over there it must be what it is like when the Australian cricket team goes over to India. People treat us like absolute superstars. They fair dinkum name their kids after Australian rugby league players. It's great to go over there and see how popular rugby league is. When you go for a drive at night, within five minutes you'll see about 50 games of footy being played on the roads by young kids.

If we are superstars over there, the PNG blokes who come over to Australia and make it in the NRL are like gods to them. There have been a few of them. Adrian Lam at the Roosters, Marcus Bai from Melbourne, David Westley and Bruce Mamando at Canberra, and a little bloke who played for the Adelaide Rams named Elias Paiyo. I remember playing against him once. I reckon he's the only player in the world who is smaller than Alfie Langer, and when I was running with the ball and saw him in front of me I thought I'd run right over the top of him. He's a strong little bloke; he picked me up so high before he dumped me that I was lucky there were no low-flying planes around. Bruce Mamando told us about the time the Kumuls were in camp preparing for a game. Paiyo was sitting down and all the PNG-based players were crowded around asking him about playing in the NRL. They all love Alfie Langer, he's like the king, and one of the Kumuls said to Paiyo, 'What's it like playing against Allan Langer?' and he said, in that PNG accent, 'Allan Langer? I threw him around like a little baby' and they all went, 'Ooooh . . .'

Anyway, that night at Townsville was a pretty tough game, even though we beat them by about 80. It was especially good for me because I scored four tries, which is a record for an Australian forward in a Test, and won the game ball. To do that in front of my old home crowd, at the Cowboys' ground, which is right next to Townsville Brothers, where I played a lot of my junior footy, made for a great memory.

We played one more warm-up game, against New Zealand Residents, and then headed over to England. Our first game was against the English at Twickenham. We got there six days early to get ready, and one day after training at the ground we had the chance to meet Prince Andrew. First off some official came out and gave us instructions on how to behave. He told us we had to call him 'Your Majesty' or 'Highness' or something. We weren't supposed to talk to him unless he talked to us first and we weren't supposed to try to shake his hand unless he offered. We said, 'Yeah sure, whatever' and got back on with training. When he arrived all the English officials lined up and he went along, all serious, shaking their hands while they bowed their heads. We kept kicking the ball around until he came over and then we just walked up and stood around him in a half circle. He'd been in the navy and the first thing he said to us was, 'So, have you had any runs ashore?' I think that meant had we had any luck with the ladies. We explained that we'd been training pretty hard and hadn't got out much and he laughed and said, 'I thought you Aussies were supposed to be able to enjoy yourselves.' We chatted for a bit longer and he seemed like a very down to earth bloke. At the time the papers over there were all full of stories about Prince Charles' son Prince William getting friendly with Britney Spears. Prince Andrew was just about to go and Michael Vella called out to him, 'Hey Andrew, has William got it on with Britney yet?' He turned and said, 'I'm his uncle. Do you tell your uncle everything you do with women?' The English officials were standing there with their jaws hitting the ground. I don't think they could believe it.

It was our turn to have our jaws hit the ground a few days later when the Englishmen got stuck into us in the first game. To say they pushed the rules as far as they could would be an understatement. They threw everything they could at us, right from the kick-off. That was fine by us. It was a good old-fashioned stoush, like the Australia–Great Britain Tests that I watched at home on the black and white telly. I had played against Great Britain once before, in the Super League Tri-Nations Test series in 1997, and having seen on TV the way Shaun Edwards cleaned up Brad Clyde in 1994, I knew they would be getting away with anything they could. When we ran out I had already decided to change the way I play just slightly. I like fighting in the tackle when I play in Australia. That way it brings a couple of extra defenders in to try to stop you picking up the extra metres or getting the ball away. With the Australian referees on the lookout for any-thing above the shoulders you are always pretty safe, but over in England I didn't think I'd risk it.

It was a pretty wise move. The rough stuff started from the kick-off. Adrian Morley just went berserk. First Robbie Kearns took the ball up and Morley cleaned him up. Then Bryan Fletcher had the ball and Morley – who was about to become Bryan's team-mate at the Roosters – belted him and broke his nose. Next was Shane Webcke's turn. He took the ball up and tried to fight in the tackle and the Poms came from everywhere to smack him. During the next passage of play I ran past him and called out, 'Hey Webbie, don't stand in the tackles with these blokes.' He turned around and there was blood pouring out of his nose and one of his eyes was half shut. He called back, 'It's a bit bloody late now.'

Harvey Howard, our Grand Final team-mate from a couple of months earlier, was playing for England. Harvey is one of the greatest characters I've ever met. I remember when we were having the big drink back at the club after the Grand Final win. Harvey disappeared for a while. Someone said, 'Where's Harvey?' and we all looked around and shrugged. About half an hour later we looked up and there he was, dressed in the total Elvis gear: white jumpsuit, sunglasses, the whole bit. Another time I was doing a Fourex promotion at the Story Bridge Hotel beer festival and there was this bloke who kept staring at me. He had the mullet haircut, a little hat, thick horn-rimmed glasses and buck teeth. It was starting to get on my nerves, and when he got up and walked over towards me I thought, here we go. Then he said, 'Hey Gordie', and it turned out to be Harvey Howard. He really made me laugh. We'd often go for a feed or a bit of a drink, and we got to be really good mates.

The first time Harvey took the ball up at Twickenham I went to tackle him and he stuck his elbow in my throat. The second time he lifted up the knee to try to hit me in the face. If I didn't know it was going to be a tough game before, I sure did then.

We won 22–2 and cruised through the early rounds. It had been a long season, so Chris Anderson told us he'd be resting a few players in some of the early matches. Wendell and I sat out our next game against Fiji, which turned out to be an interesting match because our Broncos team-mate Lote Tuqiri played. Lote was the Fijian captain, and to see the way he played, and the way he lifted his team, proved to me how important the World Cup is. Fiji would not usually get the chance to play against Australia, and Lote would not get the chance to play for his country, let alone captain them, but I reckon it was the making of him. He took on the responsibility and really led by example. He scored an unbelievable try and made some big breaks, and if he hadn't been playing the scoreline would have been about 20 points different. As it was we won 66–8, but it was a good game and the Fijians tried their guts out. That's often the way. A team plays against a much better side and the players lift. Lote sure did. Seeing him play that game was when I knew he was something special. I went into the Fijian dressing room after the match to congratulate them on a top effort. Sometimes after a team has been beaten by that much they will be very upset, and I thought I might be able to buck them up. I walked in expecting them to be down in the dumps, and they were all sitting around a guy with a guitar singing and having a great time. A couple of years ago the Broncos went to visit Lote's village on our pre-season trip to Fiji and I now know that that's just how the Fijians are. They love life. We had a great time at that village, and I'll never forget when everyone came out and farewelled us with the song 'Isa Lei'. God, it was powerful.

Our next game was against Russia, in Hull, and while it might not have been a highlight in a lot of league fans' lives, it was for me. A few days before the game Chris called Freddie Fittler and me in as captain and vice-captain to have a talk about how we thought things were going, whether we thought we needed extra training sessions and that sort of thing. Then Chris said to Freddie, 'And I think I might rest you for the Russia game.' Freddie just nodded. I looked at Freddie and said, 'Are you serious?' He said, 'Sure', and that was it. If Freddie had wanted to play Chris would have let him, but by agreeing to sit it out he was giving me the chance to captain Australia. You might say 'But it was only against Russia – and it wasn't a Test', but I couldn't care one bit. For me to captain my country was a great feeling. I know if I had retired after that game and never captained Australia again, it wouldn't have worried me at all. I'd achieved something that everyone dreams about. And even if the opposition wasn't one of the world powers in the game, there was nothing wrong with the Australian team. To look at the quality of players around me – Sailor, Webcke, Johns – and to know that I was captain of that Australian side is something I'll have with me forever. One of the things I like about playing in England is the way both teams walk out together. The thing I remember about that game is that I walked out as slowly as I could. I wanted the moment to last forever.

CHRIS ANDERSON: I had no worries at all having him as Australian captain. I know he's had hassles with referees in the past but that just doesn't come into it. He earned the job and he did it well. In some ways I'm not sure it's best for him. He's an emotional player who needs to fire up to play at his best. He needs to get on a high, and maybe being captain might hold him back a bit. That's why I try to take the pressure off him. I say to him, 'Just play your own game – that's what got you here, that's why you are captain' and he's never let me or the team down.

Our biggest scare of the tournament came in the semi-final against Wales. They led us 20–8 about ten minutes before half-time. I remember one time their hooker, Kieren Cunningham, made a break down our left side, and Freddie Fittler and I came across to tackle him. He stepped inside and made us look like schoolboys. Their five-eighth was a bloke named Lee Briers, who had played with Alf at Warrington. Alf didn't rate him too highly, and before the game he was telling Darren Lockyer, 'Look out for Lee Briers, Locky, he's pretty hot' and we all laughed. Well, you wouldn't believe it, but Briers had an absolute blinder. He put over a chip they've scored off, kicked two field goals and outjumped Locky for a high ball. So much for Alfie's scouting abilities. Luckily for us, Freddie took charge in the second half, and it was his brilliance that got us into the final against New Zealand.

After our performance against Wales in the semi, New Zealand were favourites, and that really fired us up. Everyone knows that anyone can win a one-off game. The Kiwis were match fit, and they'd been together for a month – to be honest, their form was probably better than ours. We played on Manchester United's home ground, Old Trafford, and we had Man U's dressing room. I walked in and sat in the corner. A few months later I saw a picture of David Beckham getting ready to play and he was sitting in the same spot I'd sat in. That means we've two things in common – that and our wavy hair. His is wavy blond and mine is waving goodbye.

It was raining all the way there but the playing surface itself was in great condition. Apparently they have heaters under the ground. I suppose when you've got a $100 million soccer team you don't take any chances. Speaking of which, like all English clubs, they had these huge team bathtubs in the dressing room, but they wouldn't let us use them. There were covers over them. Luckily, Old Trafford is one of the few grounds in the country with showers, which suited us a lot better anyway.

The game itself was as tough as we'd expected. It was a huge struggle which could have gone either way for a long time. Wendell had a great game and scored two tries, but it still wasn't until about 15 minutes from the end that we broke them down and moved away to win 40–12. I have to say it was a great feeling to have won. As I said, it had been a long year, and as much as happiness, I felt relief. There's a lot of pride in the Australian team. We know we are number one and we want to stay that way. We realise that eventually someone is going to beat Australia, but we don't want it to happen on our watch. That World Cup win put everyone else back in their place for another year at least.

We jumped on the bus pretty soon after the game – after all, we couldn't sit around in the team baths drinking champagne – and headed back to Leeds. We all went to the Walkabout Pub, which had been our base throughout the tournament. I've always found it funny that we travel halfway around the world and immediately try to find an Aussie bar to drink in, but given that they served Fourex on tap I didn't spend too much time thinking about it.

Later that night some of the blokes started heading off to a nightclub but it just happened that Wendell, Webbie, Locky and I stayed at the pub. That was when we talked Wendell into staying with rugby league – or thought we did.

After I'd come back from England for Mick De Vere's wedding and Christine and I had our trip to Disneyland, it was time to get ready for the 2001 season. As I've said, it was really like one long year, and while I didn't hold back during the World Cup I did try to pace myself a bit. I didn't go overboard, and I tried to have a good time as well as playing hard so I wouldn't be mentally stale by the time the home season came around. It must have worked, because I was really looking forward to the season. For one thing, it was going to be my first full season as captain. For another, I was keen to have another crack at Origin, after the disappointment of the previous year, when I'd had those problems with Harrigan and NSW scored 50 against us in the last game. I honestly almost gave it away after we lost that series.

It really hit me hard the way we had played. You never lose the passion for playing for Queensland, but for the first time I started to wonder if I wanted to go through it again. My Origin career hadn't been exactly outstanding. The first four games we'd lost, then we won in 1998, had a draw in 1999 and got flogged in 2000. I was starting to question myself, wondering if I was the problem. If we were going to go through what we had gone through in 2000 again, I wasn't looking forward to it. To tell you the truth, I was embarrassed after that series. And it didn't just affect me; it also affected people around me. Mum and Dad would cop it when they went to the shops – everyone would want to tell them where we went wrong and what we should be doing. My niece and nephew would have people coming up to them and saying things at school. That really got to me. I remember once Wayne said that when the Maroons win Origin everyone in Queensland wakes up the next morning feeling good. We take that responsibility seriously, and when we lose we feel like we've let everyone down. There's a lot of feeling there. It's just my theory, but I've always felt that when a Queenslander is picked to play Origin he's so excited because he knows he's representing Queensland, whereas I reckon there are some NSW players who are excited to be chosen because they think it might be a stepping stone to the Australian side.

I did a lot of soul-searching, and a month or so after that last Origin game I spoke to Wayne at a Broncos dinner at the Caxton Hotel. It started off with him asking me what had gone wrong, so I poured it all out. I said to him, 'Look, mate, I don't think I need it any more. I've thought it over and I think it's time to step aside, let the young blokes have a go.' I know I wear my heart on my sleeve too much, but when I said that to Wayne I really meant it. He told me he thought I had more to offer. Eventually he talked me around. I'm glad he did. If I'd walked away then it would have been a pretty miserable Origin record. Plus I would have missed out on some of the best experiences of my life.

WAYNE BENNETT: After they'd been beaten by 50 points in Origin III in 2000 there was all that drama because Queensland had just crumbled and fallen apart. They were shattered coming back, not knowing which way to turn, and I felt so guilty, because I felt I'd let them down by not coaching them. It was like when you hear the old Diggers say they feel guilty when they come back from war because they've lost their mates and can't believe they didn't die with them. For the first time I understood that feeling. I was guilty because I didn't get to share those feelings of loss with them.

About two months later I was at a function with Gorden and he opened up to me about State of Origin. He had tears in his eyes. Origin is so important and Gorden had suffered this great disappointment. He felt abandoned. The structure wasn't set up the way it should have been, and the players didn't get the support they should have. Gorden took it very personally. He felt he was to blame for the loss and he started asking himself the question: 'Why am I doing it?' It's the toughest game these blokes will ever play. They know what they have to put into it and they know they'll still be sore a month after the game. Gorden was pretty much saying, 'Is it worth it?' He was feeling that he and the rest of them weren't appreciated – not by the fans, but by the league and those people who make the decisions.

I knew how he felt, because I've felt that way myself sometimes, like you've stuck your neck out and been left to carry the can. I was older and wiser but he needed reassuring, and I needed him to know that he did have support. That pretty much clinched it for me. I knew then that I had to come back to sort things out for them. I hadn't been asked, but I knew I had to do it to make sure something like that didn't happen again. That is Gorden's passion. There is no in-between, and he brings those feelings out in other people. He's the one who brought the change. It won't really benefit him all that much – he's getting on – but it will help the younger blokes who come through. He's made sure that no-one else will ever have to carry the can like that again.

The season started well. Everything was going fine until Round 5, when I got suspended after a Friday night home game at against Newcastle. I'd tackled their forward, Steve Simpson, and come down on top of him. I was trying to put my arm out to break my fall but I missed and just clipped his forehead. Nothing more would have happened except that the *Courier-Mail* ran a picture the next day which made it look as if I was purposely trying to smash my forearm on his head. There's no way I was. If I'd wanted to do that I would have come down on the bridge of his nose, not just grazed his forehead, but the Knights were still in town waiting to catch their flight home and they read the paper. Their coach, Michael Hagan, blew up and got me cited, Steve Simpson went on about it and they put the photo in as evidence. You wouldn't believe it. I'd just started writing a column for the *Courier-Mail* and here they were helping convict me. Because I'd already been suspended for the same thing once before – the time with Martin Lang, which cost me an Origin game – I got three weeks. I still say it was a crook decision. I was disappointed with the Knights. I've always believed that what happens on the field should stay on the field. There was nothing more to that than a good hard hit, but of course because I was the one involved everything was multiplied by at least five. I admit the Martin Lang one was a fair cop, but I honestly never tried to hit Simpson.

Still, at least my being out gave Wendell his first and only game captaining the Broncos. It was against the Auckland Warriors, who had never beaten us, and Wendell ended up as the only Broncos captain ever to have a 100 per cent record. Unfortunately that's a 100 per cent losing record, but that's the way it goes.

I made my comeback with a pretty ordinary game against the Roosters, and then it was time to go in to Origin camp.

I couldn't believe how different it was from the year before. Wayne had come back as coach and the QRL had given him everything he wanted. I read in soccer player Roy Keane's book how hard it had been to go from playing for Manchester United to playing for Ireland. At Man U everything was first class, and with Ireland it was all a bit of a mess. With no disrespect to Muppet, that's how I had felt the year before. The Broncos are a totally professional outfit, and the QRL just couldn't come close. That all changed in 2001. Wayne brought in a whole new team of assistant coaches and trainers. There had been a couple of camps earlier in the year, and instead of taking us back to the Brisbane Travelodge, where every Queensland team had stayed since Wally was a boy, he took us to this place on the Gold Coast hinterland called Gwinganna Resort, a sort of a training and convention centre owned by a millionaire businessman. He brought in all these beautiful old timber buildings – even an old church – and built a little cricket field with a wooden grandstand, a pool, tennis courts and a mini golf course. The main thing about it is that it is so isolated. You get up there in a bus which climbs so high you're literally looking down on clouds and mountains. There are no pubs or nightclubs, just a rec room with a pool table and darts and board games. When I first got into Origin we spent four nights drinking beer. These days you'd be lucky to drink four beers. We spent time up at Gwinganna doing drills and talking and preparing, then we went down to a park on the Gold Coast for ball work. One of the best things is that we didn't spend much time travelling. In the Australian side it felt as if we spent most of our time sitting in buses. At Gwinganna everything we needed was there.

We had ten new faces in the side, and I felt I was part of what would be a whole new era for Queensland. Not that I had any idea what was about to happen. How could you? If someone had said to me that first day at Gwinganna, 'You'll win the first game by a lot, lose the second game by a lot and then Alfie Langer will come back from England for the third game, which you'll win', I would have laughed. It was fairytale stuff.

When we got together on the Monday and Tuesday we weren't thinking about winning that first game. No-one even mentioned the possibility. But we weren't talking about losing either. Our aim was just to get some respect back, that's all.

WAYNE BENNETT: I've seen him do so many big things on the field, but the first State of Origin in 2001 was a defining moment for me. I remember he came to me the night before the game, the Tuesday night, and he said, 'Wayne, we're going to win tomorrow.' That really impressed me, because Gordie never says anything like that. I didn't say any more about it. I think I just said, 'Okay Gorden, if you're saying that it gives me a lot of confidence.' And he did, he had a magnificent game that night. Another one was the preliminary final against Parramatta in 2000, when he scored a try that no-one else could score. And he does those things at the right time. He's the sort of player who can go into cruise control but can also sense the moment. He picks up on the urgency of the situation and he'll do what others can't.

This was supposedly the best NSW team of all time. They'd won the last series 3–nil and hammered us in game three. Then, when Australia won the World Cup, 17 of the 22 players in the squad were from NSW. They had proven that they were a very good side, so we weren't even thinking about the scoreboard. All we wanted to do was put in a gritty 80-minute Queensland performance. It just turned out to be the most special 80 minutes I've ever been involved in on a footy field. To see those young blokes from Townsville, Buttigieg and Doyle, scoring tries and Chris Walker, as Ray Warren said, 'running like a gazelle'. Or that try by Carl Webb . . . it all just proved that dreams can come true.

I've never watched a full replay of the game and I don't think I ever will. The tape will never come close to my memories. I remember that run by Lote at the start and seeing Locky come up inside him to take the pass for the try. There's so much going on during a game like that that you never think, this is great, we're on top – you just keep going, because you know they'll be back.

Later I remember Lote holding Matthew Gidley up over the line and ripping the ball off him, and thinking what a big effort it was. And I'll never forget that try by Carl Webb.

Just before half-time we were close to their line and I called for the ball. There's a bit of a pecking order in teams. If a senior player calls for it, it pretty much means they'll get it. At the Broncos it probably goes Locky, then me, then Shane Webcke. If Locky calls for the ball he'll always get it. And if a young bloke calls over the top of one of the more senior players it will usually be mentioned in the team meeting room the next week. We'll want to know why.

Anyway, there we are, pretty close to the NSW line, and

Carl Webb has sharked me. I've called for the ball and he's screamed out, 'No, give it to me', and run in front of me. Let's just say it wasn't one of his best runs. I walked past him and said, 'Hey, mate, next time you call over the top of me you'd better do more with the ball than that.' Well, next time Carl got the ball he scored one of the best tries of all time. He went one way, then the other, and bumped off and beat about five of the best defenders in the game. I've never seen anything like it in my life. As we were walking off for half-time I went over and said, 'Mate, anytime you want to call over the top of me, just go right ahead.'

Wayne was calm before the game and he was still calm at half-time, even though we were up 16–4. He said, 'You blokes have done good things, now you have to repeat them. NSW have seen what we can do, now they know what they have to do to get back into the game.' We went back out for the second half and I think John Doyle scored from the first set of tackles. I never thought it was over, and we never put the cue in the rack – we just kept going and going. I think it was only when Chris Walker scored to make it 34–4 that I realised they couldn't beat us. The thing was, NSW didn't play badly that night. It was just that five per cent I talk about.

I was walking on air after that game. The way those young blokes had stood up, the way we'd won back pride for Queensland, it was as if I'd had a shot of adrenalin that I thought would last forever. I couldn't wait for game two, couldn't wait to see what we could achieve.

Exactly two weeks later my world came crashing down.

CHAPTER THIRTEEN

A PAIN
IN THE NECK

I've never been superstitious. Maybe I should have been. I didn't even realise it was Round 13, and it didn't even cross my mind when Tony Durkin came up to me at training and suggested I should wear jersey number 13. I'd always worn number 11, but Wayne had juggled things around because someone was out. He had me, Bradley Meyers and Dane Carlaw all playing as back-rowers. None of us was really a lock, but we were sort of rotating. Durko was sending in the numbers for the program and said to me, 'Hey Gordie, I've got number 13 for you this week, big boy.' I said no, that I'd stick with 11, but he said it would be good. It would give me a new jumper for my collection. 'Yeah, all right,' I said, 'why not?'

We were playing Northern Eagles at ANZ. It had been raining on and off all day. Nothing too heavy, just enough to make the ground a little slippery. About 25 minutes into the game I went for a run down the short side. I saw Adam Muir coming across and I tried to step inside him. It was nothing spectacular, I'd done it a thousand times, but I slipped as Adam came in to tackle me and his shoulder hit my jaw. Again, no big deal. It wasn't a bad tackle. If I hadn't slipped he would have hit me right around the ball.

I wasn't knocked out, I don't think I was really even stunned, because I can remember really clearly everything that happened. I tried to get up to play the ball but I couldn't get to my feet. I sort of fell sideways and the ball slipped out of my hands. The Eagles players were calling out to the ref, 'He's dropped it, he's lost it, sir', but the ref said, 'No, I've called tackle.' See, I can remember all that, so my head was okay; I just couldn't get my body to do what I wanted it to. I managed to get halfway up and Locky came over and told me to sit down. 'You've been knocked out,' he said. I said to him, 'No, I'm okay, I'm right.' Then our trainer, Kenny Rach, came on and told me to sit down. He said, 'Come on Gordie, you've just been knocked out.' By now I was starting to get a bit pissed off that everyone was telling me I'd been knocked out. 'Mate,' I said, 'I'm not knocked out . . . I just can't feel my arms and legs.' He's just gone, '*What?*'

Locky came over and took my arm, and he and Kenny got me to my feet and started getting me off the field. I remember Locky looking at me with this strange look in his eyes. None of the boys had ever seen me going off like that before.

I must have looked pretty odd, because they were all looking at me. Ken managed to walk me over to our bench. It was really strange. My legs were getting better but it was as if the ground wasn't where I thought it was. I'd put my foot down and the ground would sort of come up to meet it.

Kenny got me on to the bench and our doctor, Peter Friis, came over and started giving me the usual little tests to see if I was concussed. Peter looked at my eyes and head. He was asking me questions – if I knew where I was and who we were playing and what tackle it was, stuff like that. It took me a while to convince him that I hadn't been knocked out and that I knew what was going on around me. I told him that I couldn't use my legs too well and I was having pins and needles in my arms. My legs were slightly better. They felt the way they do when you've sat for a long time on a bench, and my arms felt like they do when you wake up in the morning and you've slept on them. My hands were the most uncomfortable. There was this burning sensation; I had to fold my arms to try to make it go away. I sat there on the bench waiting to go back on and Peter, who was sitting about two metres away, kept staring at me and calling out questions like, 'How do your hands feel now?' After about 15 minutes I asked him if I'd be going back on. He said, 'No, mate, that's it for you today.' That was the first time I realised it might be serious. I asked him what the problem was. He said, 'Well, mate, you've got the symptoms of a spinal problem. You've had a fair whack on the neck, you'd better get it checked out tomorrow. I'll see you in my office first thing.'

That night Christine and I went out to dinner. It was her brother's birthday and we all went out for a feed. My hands were still giving me trouble. I remember I couldn't use my knife and fork too well and Christine had to ask if I wanted her to cut up my food.

CHRISTINE TALLIS: As a nurse I knew it was some kind of spinal problem because he had bilateral tingling – that is, in both hands. About a year earlier Gorden had got a knock on his neck and Peter Friis had sent him off for a scan. It showed that he had a naturally narrow spinal canal at the top of his spine, meaning he was more at risk of spinal injury than most are. I'd seen the X-rays and it was pretty obvious. I remember saying to Peter, 'How can you guarantee it won't get worse?' and he'd said, 'I can't, but you'd have to be very unlucky.'

We went home early that night because my hands were giving me so much trouble, and the next morning Christine and I went straight to St Andrews Hospital for an X-ray. Usually when I get an X-ray for a knock the bloke who does the X-ray will have a bit of a look and give me a hint before he puts it in the envelope. It's usually something like, 'Yeah, you look all right, mate' or, 'Looks like you've had a bit of a bump there.' This time he had a look and said, all serious, 'This doesn't look good.' I was still optimistic, mainly because I was walking around and everything seemed to be getting steadily better. I remember thinking, 'As long as I'm back for the third Origin.' The way I figured it, we'd won the first one and even if we lost game two in Sydney, I'd be right for the decider.

From there we went to Frissie's office at the Holy Spirit Hospital with the X-rays. He had a look, read all the mumbo jumbo and said, 'Oh. That doesn't look good.' I asked him if I'd be back for Origin. He said, 'No, Gorden. You'll be out for a while, maybe six weeks. You've had a big knock, we have to wait until these pins and needles settle down.' Peter said he wanted me to speak to a friend of his, Geoff Askin, who was a specialist in the field. His office was in the same building, so we went straight up.

By now I was starting to get a bad feeling. When it had happened I thought I would be off the field for ten minutes. Now I'd had two people tell me my X-rays didn't look good and I was being sent off to see a spinal surgeon.

Geoff Askin is a lovely bloke, but he didn't beat around the bush. He took one look at my X-rays and said what everyone else had been saying all morning: 'This doesn't look good.' He started talking about an operation and said the words 'you'll never play again'. That was when I lost it. I just started crying.

CHRISTINE TALLIS: I think he went into shock. Everything had happened so fast. He'd gone off to play football feeling fine and less than 24 hours later he was being told he needed an operation on his spine. What Geoff had done was look at the X-rays and start going through the options. The first one was do nothing, and if Gorden did that, he'd never play again. I think Gorden just picked up on those words and that's when he became emotional. But the next option was to have an operation, and depending on how it went, he might be able to play again – maybe in a year or so. There were no guarantees, though, and that was one of the things that really concerned Gorden.

If you are a footballer you'd rather get a broken arm or a broken leg than be told you might be right in such and such a time if such and such happens. With a nice clean break you're out for six weeks and that's that. With torn muscles or ligaments it could be four weeks or six or eight. Still, at least with those things you know you will be back. With me, no one was making me any promises. We were talking spinal surgery, and when that goes wrong you can end up in a wheelchair. One of the scary things for me was that just a few weeks earlier Nathan Brown had been forced to retire with a very similar problem. His spinal canal was narrow all the way down so he was in a worse situation than me, but it was still pretty freaky. You wouldn't believe it, but the four of us who knocked around in the old days at St George – me, Brownie, Jason Stevens and Craig Greenhill from Cronulla – used to play some ferocious games of beach footy on Cronulla beach back then, and all of us ended up having spinal problems. As soon as Geoff mentioned the fact that I might not play again I thought of Brownie. It wasn't a good thought. Geoff gave us some broad details about the operation and arranged for me to see a neurologist the next day. Things were going from bad to worse.

At least this bloke didn't look at the X-rays and say, 'This doesn't look good'. It was a lot worse than that. He sat me down and told me to close my eyes and put my hands out. Then he started putting things in my hands. He might put a piece of cotton wool there. The next time he'd scratch me with a pin or put something cold or hot there. The trouble was, I didn't have a clue what he was doing, none at all. He could have put a porcupine there and I wouldn't have known.

CHRISTINE TALLIS: That was the worst. To see Gorden sitting there with his eyes closed not knowing what was being put in his hands was very hard to watch. I was trying not to break down and cry. Being a nurse, I'm the one that Gorden looked to for reassurance. As soon as the doctor told him to open his eyes he looked over at me to see what I thought. I had to stay calm, but it was one of the hardest things I've ever had to do. It was a very scary time.

When I finished the test the doctor looked at me and said, 'You are a very lucky man to be sitting here talking to me. Have you achieved everything you want to in your game?'

How do you answer that? I was thinking, yeah, I've played for my country and state, I've won Grand Finals – but is that all? I wanted to play football, I wanted to be around my mates and live the life I enjoyed living. I wasn't thinking about the money, but playing football was the only thing I'd ever done in my life. I wasn't sure what I'd do if I couldn't play any more. Most footy players know when they are going to retire. You work it out and sign your last contract so you finish when you're around 32, maybe older if you're lucky, but you are prepared for it. I was 28, but I didn't feel 28. I felt it was too early to be giving up something I loved so much, something that was such a big part of my life. I wasn't ready. The doctor said to me, 'I'd be retiring if I were you.'

That was some couple of days. The first doctor said I'd be out for six weeks, the second said a year at best and the third said I should retire. I was glad I didn't have to see a fourth doctor. I think he would have had me six feet under.

Chris and I got into the car and went over to Mum's, and on the way I rang Wayne Bennett on the mobile. Wayne was at his farm. Everyone knows he goes there to relax on Tuesdays and you don't ring him at the farm, but I thought this was important enough to disturb him. I was pretty emotional. I'd just been made captain and I felt I was letting him and everyone else down. I said to him, 'Wayne, I've got some bad news. I can't play again this year.'

He said, 'That's all right, mate. Your health is more important than football. Just make sure you get right.' I told him they were talking about operating, taking some bone from my hip and grafting it onto my spine. I said to him, 'They're saying I might never play again.'

'What's wrong with that?' he said. 'Gorden, as long as you can walk, that's the main thing. You just do what has to be done and do it as quick as you can. The longer you wait the less chance you have of getting better.'

The way Wayne handled it made me feel a lot better. I had already made up my mind to have the operation, but in a funny sort of way I kept thinking I might not need it. I really thought I might just get better by myself. My hands were getting steadily better but I think I was fooling myself by thinking that I was recovering faster than I was.

A few days after seeing all the doctors my family came around to my place for breakfast. Christine put some eggs on the stove to boil and everyone was fussing around in the kitchen making toast and stuff. Someone got the eggs out of the water and I went over and started peeling them. Mum took one from me and dropped it immediately and stuck her hand under the cold water tap. 'Gorden,' she said, 'How can you hold this? It's burning.' Everyone looked down at my hands as I just stood there holding these boiling eggs. I honestly couldn't feel a thing. I think that was when we all realised just how bad things were.

We kept it quiet for a week because we didn't want it in the press. I went along to watch the boys play their next game and in the dressing room afterwards Wayne told them. He said, 'Listen, boys, you'll read it in the paper tomorrow, but Gorden's not going to be playing for us again this year and we don't know what his future is going to be. He's got to have a delicate operation and we're all hoping it works out.'

I couldn't say anything to them. I didn't know if I'd be able to keep it all in. It was bad enough looking at their faces. You hate to see your mates injured and this was one right out of the box.

Over the next week or so I had about three meetings with Dr Askin. He was sensational. Some doctors go on with all the technical stuff and you can't understand what they are talking about, but Geoff made it all very clear. He explained that due to the impact of the tackle a disc at the top of my spine had been pushed into the narrowed part of my spinal canal and was putting pressure on my spinal cord. That was what was giving me the pins and needles and affecting my movement. He said he was going to take out the disc and fuse two of my vertebrae together using some bone they'd take from my hip. Then they'd join it all together with a titanium plate. He said with older people they sometimes use cow bones, which they have to get from overseas, but because I was young, some of my own bone would heal faster. I was happy with that, because I thought the cow bone might moove around a bit.

I can laugh about it now, but when he was telling me about it I was scared stiff. Especially when he described how they were going to do it. They cut your throat open, push your voice box aside and go in from the front. Try staying calm when someone you've hardly met before tells you they're going to do that to you. I asked him again if I'd be able to play and he said again that he couldn't say whether I'd come back 100 per cent. If the spinal cord was damaged there would be nothing he could do about it, but my hands kept improving and he told me that was a good sign. When it had first happened the whole of my arms were sore. Then it had been as if I was wearing gloves, and finally it was just the three big fingers on each hand. Geoff said that was promising. Of course there was another thing to worry about too: in some cases the voice box is damaged, so I might not be able to talk properly again.

I shouldn't have worried, though. Everyone from Peter

Friis down was telling me how good Geoff was. All the doctors at the hospital where Christine worked asked who was doing the operation, and when she told them they'd say, 'He's the best.' Even when I was in the prep room waiting to go into surgery a nurse came in and told me not to worry, that I had a good doctor.

The fact that I could even talk to that nurse was another story. I've had my share of small operations, and in every one the nurse will come into my room beforehand and give me a shot so that I'm nice and relaxed by the time I get into the prep room. Usually I'm so zonked I can't stay awake. Not this time. I had the shot but it didn't affect me. It might have been because of my nerves, but I was wide awake. Geez, I was scared. They gave me one of those little shower caps to wear and handed me some paper underpants. I remember thinking as I put them on, 'The way I'm feeling I don't think these are going to be strong enough.' Then they wheeled me down the corridor and people were saying, 'Good luck, Gorden, you'll be right.' I should have been out to it but I was waving back and talking to them. Then when I got into the prep room a nurse came up and asked how I was. I told her I was fine and then she pulled out some footy cards and asked me to sign them. Maybe she thought they'd be worth a lot of money if I didn't pull through. The club's orthopaedic surgeon, Peter Myers, dropped in too. He could tell I was nervous. He said, 'Don't worry, you're in good hands. I'm just doing a knee next door. It won't take long. As soon as I'm finished I'll come in and watch, if you like.' Finally Geoff walked in. I remembered something that had been bothering me. I asked him if I would need to walk around in one of those frames with the steel bolts to take pressure off my neck while it healed. He said to me, 'Gorden, when I'm finished you can jump out the window and where I put that plate will be the only part that isn't damaged. It'll be the strongest part of your body.' Then they put me to sleep.

When I woke up at six o'clock the first thing I noticed was that I could move my neck. I thought it would be the part that hurt me but it didn't bother me at all. My throat was a bit sore where they'd cut me open and my hip hurt, but that made sense. The neck was the thing that surprised me. And then I realised my hands didn't have any pins and needles any more. It was instantaneous. Completely gone. When I told Geoff that he was really happy. He said the operation had gone very well, but the no pins and needles were the best sign.

When a nurse came in I asked her if I could get out of bed and go for a walk. She said I could try if I wanted to. They gave me one of those walking frames with the wheels on it and I was going down the corridor when this little old lady came after me with her walking frame. I'd given her about five metres start but she caught me. I tried to put in the big ones but I couldn't keep up with her. That's when I thought I'd better conserve my strength for a while. I didn't want all the old dears taking me on and boasting to their friends that they'd beaten Gorden Tallis in a sprint.

The next day Durko came in and told me that the media was camped outside the hospital trying to find out about me and ringing up my family and the club all the time. He asked if I wanted to talk to them and Geoff said it was okay with him if it was okay with me. To be honest, I just saw it as an opportunity to get out of bed again. As long as none of the old ladies were hanging around outside on their walking frames, I was happy to do it. We called all the media to the hospital and I went out and talked to them for about ten minutes before my voice started to go. I guess I was more tired than I thought, but all the blokes from the media were great. They appreciated what we'd done for them and no-one tried to make me do more than I could. After that I just collapsed back in my bed. I was exhausted.

By then the main problem was my throat. My voice was all hoarse and I could hardly swallow. All I could eat was jelly and custard and I was finding it hard to get my tablets down. That afternoon I was lying in bed half asleep and this nurse came in with a big tablet. She said to me, 'Could you tuck your knees up for me please, Gorden.' I didn't know what she wanted, so I just did it and whooshka, she's stuck that big tablet right up my you-know-what. The next morning when I woke up this male nurse has come in with another one of those big tablets. He's said, 'And how are you today, Gorden?' Well, I sat bolt upright and said, 'Mate, I'm great, never better. Listen, would you just leave that tablet here? My wife's a nurse and she'll be in any minute now. We'll work it out.' As soon as he left I chucked the tablet into the bin and I never took another one as long as I was there.

From day one, I just couldn't believe how many flowers and cards people were sending. It was amazing. The room was full of flowers and more kept coming every day. Every night I'd ask the nurses to take some home with them and the next morning the room would be full again. The mail-man must have given himself a hernia bringing the cards up and the phone never stopped ringing. I got messages from the Prime Minister and Premier Beattie. Paul Kelly, the captain of the Sydney Swans, rang and I got a call from Pat

Rafter in the US. When that sort of stuff happens you just can't believe how many people care about you and you can't help feeling humble. You think, where did this all come from? Sometimes in this game you cop a lot, but you also get a lot of support. You just have to take the good with the bad.

I was out of there a few days later, and from there on it was just a slow process of check-ups and X-rays. After three weeks I had the first scan and Geoff said everything was fine. The metal plate was all in place and looking strong. He said as long as my hip cleared up I could start doing light weights in six weeks.

Before I did that I went down to Sydney for the second Origin. It was very hard in a lot of ways. First, because I wanted to be playing so much, second, because the boys lost, and third, because I sat with Wayne. You reckon the players cop a hard time? You should see what the coaches go through. We were sitting in an open box at the Olympic Stadium and the crowd was just giving it to Wayne. It was like, 'You arsehole, Bennett', and worse from the second we walked in. The Blues really gave it to us that night, and every time they scored, the crowd in front of us would turn around and scream abuse and give him the finger. Wayne just ignored it, but I had steam coming out of my ears. I was trying to stare them down, thinking, you dickheads, have some respect. I remember thinking it was easier to be out in the middle than in the stands.

It was after that loss in game two, of course, that Wayne brought Alf back from England to play. Wayne rang Alf in Warrington and the first thing Alf said was, 'What took you so long?' Again, the third Origin game was very hard to sit through. I'd been with the team up at Gwinganna and to be there and not be part of it all was pretty difficult. I would have done anything to be part of that amazing game with Alfie, but it just wasn't to be.

WAYNE BENNETT: After we lost the second game, I needed an inspirational player. It's hard to say whether I still would have brought Alfie back from England if Gorden hadn't been hurt but we had a lot of kids in that team and I needed someone they would follow. They would have followed Darren Lockyer, but I needed someone in the centre of the park. In a situation like that if you can't have Gorden Tallis there's only one other person, and that's Alfie.

After we won game three and sewed up the Origin I felt I had to get away. Geoff had told me I couldn't do any contact work for 12 weeks, and it was pretty painful just showing up at training every day and watching the boys run around. Our next door neighbour was going to Finland and asked us to come along. I asked Wayne if I could go and he said, 'Why not? You'll only be annoying me hanging around here.'

Finland was good, and we went to the Greek Islands as well, where I survived a fitness test on my neck by falling off a donkey, but the highlight for me was going to Wimbledon. When Pat Rafter had rung a couple of weeks earlier I'd told him that I'd like to come over to watch him and he said I should, so I did. Pat had given me the number of the place where he was staying and I gave him a call. I spoke to his brother and he arranged some tickets with the rest of them for the semi-final. Pat won, and when the game finished he turned and pointed at us in the stands, then hit a ball up to us. I was sitting next to the bloke who travels around the world with Pat and picks up his balls and racquets after practice. Pat hit the ball and this bloke caught it. I thought, 'How good is this? I'll get it off him and have Pat sign it.' And then the bloke threw it straight back down onto the court. I said, 'Mate, it's all right for you . . .'

After I got back to Australia I got another chance to spend some time with Pat, when he came along to watch us play St George in the preliminary final. He was in Sydney with the Davis Cup team and he brought them along to dinner with us the night before the game. Pat is a big Broncos fan and Wally Masur has been a St George supporter all his life. Lleyton Hewitt doesn't know much about rugby league. He wanted to go along with Pat, but Wally made him wear a St George jersey to the game and took him into the St George dressing room. It made for a pretty funny night.

We won that game, which put us into the final against Parramatta, but Carl Webb pulled his hamstring. By then it was 17 weeks since my operation. At 12 weeks Geoff had said I could do anything at training, just no heavy contact work. Now here it was five weeks later and I'd started picking up the intensity. I still hadn't done any straight out one-on-one tackling but I was working on the pads: holding them as the big blokes like Webbie ran into me and doing the same to them. That week at training I heard Wayne and Craig Bellamy talking about what they would do to cover Carl in the Parramatta game. They thought he might be able to get through some of the game but they couldn't risk him for all of it. I said, 'Wayne, I'll play.' He said, 'Don't be stupid.' I said, 'Wayne, I'll play.' Something in the way I said it made him realise I was serious. He asked me what the doctor would say.

'There's no harm in asking him,' I said. 'It's been 17 weeks and I'm getting smashed by Webbie at training. As long as I don't get hit in a head-high I'll be okay.' I thought maybe Carl could go on for 25 minutes each half and I could come on for the last 15 minutes. I knew I could last 15 minutes. I rang Geoff first thing the next morning. He was expecting it. 'I knew you'd call,' he said. 'Let me talk to a few people. I'll get back to you.'

When I went to training that afternoon there must have been something about the way I threw myself into it. A couple of reporters came up afterwards and asked me if there was any chance I would be playing. One asked if I had thought about asking my doctor. I couldn't tell a lie. 'I'm ahead of you fellas,' I said. 'I've already asked him. He's giving me an answer tomorrow.' What I didn't know was that Geoff had been operating all that day and didn't have a chance to call me. In the meantime it had blown up. All the papers, radio talkback and TV news were getting stuck in.

CHRISTINE TALLIS: I wasn't particularly worried, because I knew Geoff wouldn't let him. I just said to him, 'Don't get your hopes up, Gorden.' I knew it probably wouldn't happen. I just didn't want to see him let down.

Some people in the media were saying it was all a con by Wayne to upset Brian Smith's preparation, but it disturbed us more than him because we couldn't decide on a team. Finally Geoff rang back. He said, 'Haven't you caused a ruckus.' Then he told me why he hadn't called earlier and said, 'I think we'll give it a miss.' That was it. There was nothing I could do except keep up with the exercises the physio had given me to strengthen my neck muscles and get ready for 2002.

WAYNE BENNETT: My involvement in his comeback from the neck injury was very low key. My concern is always with the player and life after football. I didn't want to put pressure on him and make him feel he owed the club anything. I didn't want him to feel guilty. He'd seen his mate Nathan Brown's career finish prematurely, so my role was just to be there and support him if he needed me. I was like a father confessor.

In the end I decided to wait until the absolute last minute before going to see Geoff to get a clearance for the 2002 season. There was a Saturday night trial against Canterbury at Toowoomba and I went to see Geoff on the Thursday. Before the final against Parramatta the year before I'd been pretty calm when I'd rung him. It was like a gamble. I knew he probably wouldn't let me play but I had nothing to lose by asking. This was different. This was the rest of my career, and I was shaking. As I waited to go into his office I could have done with a few pairs of those paper underpants. He asked me how I was feeling, how my weight was. Then he said the words I had been waiting almost a year to hear.

'Well,' he said, 'I can't see any reason why you shouldn't play.'

I didn't think about it much when I got ready for that game at Toowoomba. I certainly didn't think about what could happen if something went wrong. All I did was tell myself that I'd be the one in charge. I decided that when I did get involved in the game it would be at a time and place of my choosing. And when I did make a run I was going to make sure it was at the smallest bloke on the field.

It was a miserable night, cold and foggy. I don't know how many people were there, but it wasn't many. Even Wayne wasn't there. He'd split the squad into two and he was with the others, who were playing somewhere else. Alfie was making his comeback in the same game as me. I played for 20 minutes, and when I finally got the ball I went for a little run and got tackled. I didn't score, I didn't even run very far, and we got beaten by about 50. But I was back. That was all I cared about. I was back.

CHAPTER FOURTEEN

BAD SIGN

Lote saw it first. We'd just run out for the final Origin game of 2002 at Stadium Australia in Sydney. Lote plays on the left wing and I stand just in front of him for kick-offs. We were headed back to our positions and he said to me, 'Geez, Gordie, look at that. Don't let them do this to you, mate.' I looked over and saw a giant sign being held up in the crowd. It said something about my mother. There has been some debate over what it said or what it actually meant, but I don't give a damn about that. All I know is that it was about my mother and she was sitting in the stand.

There's nothing new about me copping a hard time from

the crowd. As I've said earlier, they can say anything they like about me. I reckon I've heard it all. 'Get off the steroids, Gordie', 'Get back in your tree, you black bastard.' You name it, someone has shouted it and I cop it sweet. Sometimes it's even funny, and I might give a little bit back. In Round 2, 2003, against Souths at the Sydney Football Stadium, the crowd was really giving it to me. I'd had that fight with Ben Ross from Penrith the week before and the media was going on about how I was a thug. Before the game I was signing autographs for some kids and a Souths supporter screamed out, 'Watch out he doesn't punch you, kid.' Once the game started they were right into me, especially when Souths looked like pulling off an upset. Midway through the second half I scored a try and when I walked back to halfway I put my hand behind my ear, like, 'I can't hear you', and they went berserk, screaming abuse. A little while later I put through a freak grubber for Michael De Vere to score and I put the hand behind the ear again. The abuse wasn't quite as loud but it was still there. And then, right on full-time, when all they had to do was hold on to the ball in the last tackle to win, I ripped the ball out and we won with eight seconds to go. This time when I put the hand behind the ear I couldn't hear a thing. Maybe they were all too busy crying. So as you can see, I think it's all part of the game. The more involved the fans are the better, as far as I'm concerned. As long as they don't throw things or spit on me like the Penrith fans did after the Ben Ross fight, I don't have a problem.

I couldn't believe security didn't do something about it that night, especially when you think of what they do at the cricket when someone bounces a beach ball around to get everyone involved. Security reacts as if it's a bomb or something. They come from everywhere and put a hole in it and sometimes people get thrown out of the ground. But here we had a sign that I personally found offensive, in view of everyone, and security walked past as if it didn't exist.

The funny thing is, whoever wrote that sign probably did me a favour. Not that I needed any more motivation, but it certainly fired me up. We'd lost the first game in Sydney 32–4, with Andrew Johns doing what he said he was going to do – dominate. I'd thought he was a bit silly saying that, especially when he said he wanted to dominate the way Wally Lewis had in the 1980s. To me there will only ever be one Wally, and saying something like that just sets you up to look silly, but to his credit, Andrew was too good for us that night. That was the game when the Sydney press had called us Dad's Army and put a photo of us in old uniforms on the back page of the paper. It was also the game where Bill Harrigan sent me to the sin-bin. I remember after the game I went to the media conference, and when I came back there was a 10 or 12-year-old kid standing in the tunnel outside our dressing room. That's pretty unusual, so I just assumed he must be the nephew of one of the players or maybe a son of a trainer or something. I said hi and asked him if he wanted to come in and get some autographs. He said he did so I took him in and got some of the boys to sign his program. Then our assistant coach, Gary Belcher, came up and said, 'That's Bill Harrigan's son.' I said to him, 'Hey, kid, what did you think of your dad's performance tonight?' He said, 'Not much. He shouldn't have sent you off.' I patted him on the head and said, 'Now you be sure to tell your dad that before you go to bed tonight, won't you.'

For game two, at ANZ, we had to get back to basics. In State of Origin that means playing like Queenslanders. To borrow a quote from soccer player Roy Keane, who was born in Cork, Ireland, and said 'I'm an Irishman by birth but a Corkman by blood', I'm an Australian by birth but a Queenslander by blood. I'm pretty sure that's how we all feel when we play State of Origin. We know we will never outscore NSW at Origin. We will never outplay them at their game, they are just too brilliant. They have the best players in the game, like Laurie Daley and Brad Fittler and Andrew Johns. Just look at the Test sides. No matter who has won the Origin series, NSW will always have about 12 players in the squad and Queensland five. So we won't ever come close when it comes to throwing the ball around or putting on the fancy moves. What we can do is out-guts them, out-enthuse them. Grind our noses in front and stay there, and never give up until the final whistle. Of course that had been the plan in game one too, but they had beaten us to the punch. Gus had worked out a good match plan and they stuck to it perfectly, running us off our feet, so it was back to the drawing board.

What we had to do for game two was pull them into the trenches, play them at our game, not theirs. And that's pretty well exactly how it happened. Lote had a blinder, scoring three tries and three goals, and Dane Carlaw and I got one each. But no matter how many points anyone else scored, that game was always going to be remembered for the two passes Justin Hodges threw in our in-goal, which led to NSW tries. It can be a cruel game – as they say, a game of inches. If that first pass he threw to Locky had stuck and Locky had got out of the in-goal the commentators would have been saying, 'Oh what great vision from a young man in his first Origin game. What confidence. He's prepared to have a go.' Instead everyone was bagging him.

The first time it happened I walked up to him and said, 'Keep your head up mate, don't worry about it. Just keep looking forward.' The second time I didn't get a chance to say anything. I just looked at him in disbelief, and by the time I could think of something to say Wayne had taken him off.

You've got to hand it to Justin, though. He came back stronger every game he played from then on. It was a hard time for him but he won a Grand Final and played superbly in the World Club Championship game against St Helens. The thing is, when you think about it, Locky had a similar debut for Australia and Lote's first game in the top grade for the Broncos wasn't much better, but they all came back and showed their class. It just shows you how hard it is to play fullback or wing in your first big game. It's odds-on that the coach or captain of the opposition team is going to send up the bombs to test you out, and at that level the kickers can put it on a sixpence. In those positions you are on your own, with nowhere to hide. They can have fullback and wing to themselves, thanks.

Which brings us back to game three and that sign. I was furious. It probably wouldn't worry my mother, but I was feeling bad for her and for Christine, who was sitting with her. I would have liked to climb the fence, rip the sign down and feed it to the bloke who wrote it but I couldn't. All I could do was throw myself into the game.

It was a typical Origin match in everything but the result. I remember at the media conference before the game someone had said something about Queensland only needing to draw to win the series because we held the trophy. We knew those were the rules, and so did NSW, but I said something like, 'Yeah, good chance of that. There's only been one draw in 20 years so I can't see it happening.' Guess that's why I'm a lousy punter.

When Darren Lockyer 'scored' with about ten minutes to go I thought we were home and hosed but when it took so long for the video ref to make up his mind I started to worry. I couldn't believe it when that try was disallowed. You didn't even have to be an expert to know it was a try. You could get someone from anywhere in the world who had never even heard of rugby league, give them a rule book and they'd know that was a try. But the video ref said no try and the Blues scored five minutes later to hit the front. Then, right on full-time, Dane Carlaw scored that incredible try to square the series.

That was when I walked over towards the sign and gave it to the bloke holding it up. If Dane had scored the try any-where else but in that corner; if we'd been running the other direction, I never would have done it. It was just one of those things. I had been following the direction of play and that took me right over to where the sign was. It was just a natu-ral reaction. I'm sorry it was on TV. Obviously I had no idea it was, but I don't regret it one bit. Any person worth their salt would stick up for themselves in a situation like that. There was a lot of emotion there; the emotion of the series, of winning the game and of this bloke insulting my family. It probably took three seconds, and then I went over to the rest of my team to celebrate.

You could tell from the way we were jumping around that we knew we'd kept the title. You don't hug each other like that when you've drawn a match with a kick to come. The kick was meaningless. I'll let you into a secret. I almost walked over and took the kick myself – and miss it on purpose – because I wanted the crowd to know we didn't care if it went over or not. In the end I decided not to because I didn't want to make a fuss. If I'd known how much fuss was coming any-way I wouldn't have worried.

Afterwards, as I got ready to step up and get the trophy, Geoff Carr came up to me and said, 'Look, mate, when you get up on stage would you mind asking Andrew Johns to come up too? That would be a nice gesture coming from you.' I know I would be embarrassed if it had happened the other way around. I wouldn't have gone up, and I felt embarrassed for Andrew. It was just a PR stunt to keep everyone happy because the game was in Sydney. I just shrugged when Geoff asked me but there was no way I was going to make out it was my idea because I wouldn't insult Andrew like that. I said, 'The ARL has asked me to ask Andrew Johns to come up here too.' I don't think he looked too comfortable. The selectors were picking a team to play Great Britain in two weeks time and with Freddie Fittler retiring from representative football most judges had the captaincy between Andrew Johns and me. I had been vice-captain to Freddie, and Queensland had just won the Origin, but I knew the push from NSW would be for Andrew. When he got up on the stage I whispered to him, 'I think they just wanted the Australian captain up here.'

When I walked off the field I went straight to Mum and Christine, and gave Christine a kiss. Then I turned to Mum and I was still so upset I had tears in my eyes. I said, 'Did you see it, Mum?' and she said, 'See what?' I was going to tell her but Wayne was behind me and he just pushed me down the tunnel. 'Mate,' he said, 'she didn't see it. Don't bring it up, just keep walking.'

WAYNE BENNETT: His mother is a huge influence on him. She's the one who gets him going. We played terribly in the first State of Origin in 2002 so I got to him the day before game two. I know how to rev him up. I don't do it too often, but when I do I let him have it. I told him the facts of life and he looked at me for a while and said, 'Well I won't have to ring Mum tonight.' I took that as a compliment.

I thought that was the end of it, but Channel 9 producer Glenn Pallister came up to me in the dressing room and said, 'Gordie, do you want to give us your side of it?' I didn't know what he was talking about. Then a newspaper reporter came in and said, 'Mate, there's going to be huge headlines tomorrow about you giving it to the crowd.' That's when I realised it must have been on TV. I was still genuinely upset about it and I said to the reporter, 'Mate, you saw that sign. What would you have done in my position?' He said he'd do exactly what I'd done. I said to him, 'Well, why don't you write that then? Why don't you write the truth?' He said his editor wasn't interested. I asked him for his mobile phone and said, 'Come on, I'll ring your editor right now and ask him what he would have done in my place', but he wouldn't be in it so I told him to get away from me before I really got angry. That's when I went over and recorded the interview with Andrew Voss for Glenn Pallister.

The Sydney media really went to town. They reckoned it just proved that I couldn't be Australian captain because I couldn't control my emotions. The Sydney papers and TV stations went out and interviewed the mother of the bloke with the sign. Durko rang me and told me the papers were trying to get me and the kid together for a kiss and make up photo. I told him there was no way I would be in it. I didn't want to shake his hand, I just wanted the whole thing to go away, but of course the media down there tried to keep it going as long as they could rather than let something negative simply fade away. People were saying my reaction was a bad thing for kids to see, but I couldn't help thinking, what's worse, my reaction or the sign in the first place?

The next night they aired the interview I did in the dressing room on *The Footy Show* and even though I'm not much of a talker, I reckon that night I went pretty well. Andrew Voss was interviewing me and he asked me if I was upset that the incident could ruin my chances of being Australian captain. I said, 'Listen, it would be great to be Australian captain, it would be a great honour, but if they don't pick me because I have strong family values and stick up for my mum, then I don't want to be captain.'

After that, it was as if I'd got a whole new fan base. I got so many mothers and grandmothers coming up and saying how much they respected what I'd done that I thought I should have done it earlier. One grandmother came up to me and said she'd be proud to have me for a son. I take that as a great compliment.

WAYNE BENNETT: He's a great man. What pisses me off is when the media and the administrators try to pull him down. We can't get enough of his type of guy in sport and people want to bring him down. It hurts him – if he says it doesn't, he's just covering up. He moves on, but it does hurt him.

Like that business with the sign in the crowd. He couldn't understand why people were criticising him – he'd been doing that all his life. It was, 'If you put shit on my friends, if you put shit on my family, you're putting shit on me – and I'm going to do something about it.' That's his code. To him, that's what being a man is; if you can't do it, you're not being a man.

After all that, I wasn't surprised when they gave Andrew the Australian captaincy. Actually, even if that kid hadn't held that sign up in the crowd I wouldn't have got the job. I never really thought I was a chance. To tell the truth, if I was a selector I would have given it to Andrew too. Let's be honest, he's the best player in the world and the media was behind him. Plus he's from NSW. Personality-wise there probably wasn't much in it. As the Sydney papers pointed out, Andrew gets into trouble off the field and I get into trouble on the field. Personally, I know where I'd rather get into trouble, but that's just my opinion. Age is another big thing. I've got two, maybe three years left in the game, Andrew has five. Barring injury he is going to be at the helm a lot longer than me so it's the smart move to have him.

There was another thing too. My form. It wasn't my best year. As a matter of fact, I thought I had a shocker. It was during that year that I could really see where Alfie was coming from in 1999 when he retired for the first time. We thought he was going okay but he knew he wasn't playing to his own standards. It was the same with me. I know what I should be doing and that year I just wasn't doing it. People would tell me I was playing well but I knew I wasn't. Even the statistics lied. If you look at my numbers for the year they'll be pretty good. In one game I think I did 22 hit-ups and 20 tackles, which looks great on paper, but it's a case of quantity, not quality. In how many of those hit-ups did I make a break or suck in three or four defenders? In how many of those tackles did I knock someone back five metres or really hurt them? Not many, I'd reckon. There weren't a lot of games that season where I walked off feeling good about myself.

I think it all started to go bad in Round 2. We played the Bulldogs at ANZ and drew 20–all. It was a wet night and I got hit high more than I thought I should. There probably wasn't anything in it, but I got it into my mind that they were targeting my neck, trying to test out the injury. By the end of the game my neck was absolutely killing me and I couldn't help but be worried. I thought I'd re-injured it. At full-time their prop, Mark O'Meley, came over to shake my hand and I just brushed him. He told his captain, Steve Price, and Pricey, who is a mate of mine from Origin, came up and said, 'What's up with you?' I told him, and I could tell he was shocked I'd even think they'd do that to me, but that's how I was then. I took it personally and was really dirty about it.

The next day I went to get X-rays and headed straight to Geoff Askin's office. I told him that my neck was really sore and that I was worried. Those seconds as he looked at the scans seemed like hours, but he said everything was fine. 'As long as your neck is hurting you know it's not your spine,' he said. 'If you get the pins and needles in your hands again, that's when you have to worry.' Geoff said the spot where he had fused my vertebrae together was stronger than it had ever been, but I have to say it didn't really put my mind at rest. My confidence was down and it didn't recover for a long time.

WAYNE BENNETT: He didn't think he had the best year in 2002 but we didn't have any complaints. It is just the standard he sets for himself, and he never stopped trying. That year, against Penrith, Scott Sattler knocked him out. Shoulder under the jaw. Gorden thought it was a cheap shot. He went back into the line, dazed but coherent, and he told the trainer he was right to stay on. He got the ball about 30 metres out from our line and he just charged straight at Scott Sattler and went over the top of him. He went 70 metres, beating the fullback. The winger caught him right on the tryline but Gorden went over for the try. It was just a show of aggressive force and power; Gorden at his fiercest because he had been stung and hurt. It was that thing in his shirt that a coach can't give; you've either got it or you haven't. He'd been knocked down, but he got up and dusted himself off and gave it straight back. And the thing was, after the try Craig Bellamy got a message to me that Gorden had no idea what he had just done. He was still in a daze from the knock but his subconscious had taken over. The thing inside him which makes him a champion had come out. I said to Craig, 'Leave him there. He's been thinking too much lately anyway.'

There's really only one premiership game I can look back on from that season and feel happy about, and that was the qualifying final against Parramatta. I had plenty of incentive to do well against the Eels because of what had happened in the first round, with Brian Smith sending out his team to con the referee into sending me off. Plus there was a lot of talk that the Broncos were out of form and Parramatta would flog us. Even all that wasn't enough. I wanted to gee myself up more, and that's how I came up with the white boots.

It all started when I was watching the soccer World Cup on TV and saw that Korea were wearing white boots. I mentioned to the Nike rep that I thought they looked good, and next thing I know a pair arrived at my home with the 'Raging Bull' logo on the tongue. All my boots have the 'Raging Bull' logo on them, much to the amusement of my teammates. The first time he noticed it Wayne started chuckling and calling me 'The Raging Poddy Calf'. He thought that was so clever that he said it every time he saw me putting my boots on.

I thought the white ones looked great, but I never thought about wearing them in a game. We'd been through it all before with Wendell, when he announced he was going to wear silver boots in the 2000 Grand Final. I don't know if he ever really thought he'd go through with it, but it got a fair bit of publicity at the time. Everyone knows the story of Graeme Langlands wearing white boots and having a shocker in the 1975 Grand Final against Easts, and as we were also playing the Roosters that year it created a bit of a stir.

On the Thursday night before that 2000 Grand Final we had all gone out for a bit of a relaxing drink at The Rocks.

No-one had said much about Wendell wearing the silver boots, but after a couple of beers I couldn't help myself. As I said earlier, I'm not superstitious, but we had all worked so hard to get to the Grand Final I just didn't want anyone to put more pressure on themselves or the rest of us. I said, 'Dell, don't wear them. If you want to wear silver boots, fine, wear them in the World Cup, but don't wear them in the Grand Final.' Wendell's big saying that year was 'Beat it', which is what he said to me then. But if he thought that was the end of it, he was mistaken. As soon as he said it, everyone was into him. I didn't realise that everyone else felt the same way I did, but having come so far we didn't want to jinx ourselves. To his credit, much as he might have wanted to wear them, Wendell went with the team and left the silver boots in his hotel room.

The qualifying final against Parramatta in 2002 was different. It wasn't the Grand Final, and no matter what the result, we'd still have another game. I don't know when I first thought of wearing those boots, but after the season I'd had I knew I needed something extra, some boost to make me have a big one against the Eels.

Step one was getting it past Wayne. That was easy. I had them outside my locker after training one day and he said, 'Geez, that's a nice boot.' I told him I was thinking of wearing them. 'Why don't you?' he said. After that I took them with us when we went into camp on the Gold Coast. One night I was lying in bed and I looked at them and just thought, 'Bugger it. I'm going to wear them.' The next day I took them with me to training and while everyone gave me a bit of a hard time about 'The Raging Poddy Calf' white boots, no-one seemed too worried. Then, as we were getting ready to go back to our hotel, Corey Parker came up to me. Corey is a really old-fashioned kid. He's a Beaudesert boy who grew up tough. Just like the way he plays the game – straight up the middle – he doesn't go for the fancy trimmings. 'Gordie,' he said, 'Don't wear 'em, mate.' I put my hand on his shoulder and said, 'I'm not doing this to put pressure on you, Corey. I'm doing it to put pressure on myself. I'll be right.' Whether it was the white boots or not I don't know, but I finally got to walk off the field after a game in 2002 feeling I'd done my job.

DAVID MIDDLETON, Rugby League Yearbook 2003: *It was a bitter blow for the Eels, who were a chance of continuing a remarkable record at ANZ Stadium until a try to Tallis 12 minutes from fulltime. The Broncos captain had spent a short time on the interchange bench but returned to make a giant impact late in the game. The return of Tallis after a nine-minute rest was the turning point of the match. Often criticised in 2002 for not producing the impact he had in previous seasons, Tallis turned in a superb display. He hit the line hard and often and contributed heavily to his team's defensive effort.*

The next week we played the Roosters for the chance to go into the Grand Final. Alfie was crook; he really shouldn't have played, because he spent the entire week in the physio's room getting treatment on his leg. It was a game which we could have won, but my old mate Bill Harrigan certainly wasn't doing us any favours. The penalties were 8–1 to the Roosters before we got one right at the death. By then it was all over. One of Alfie's last ever passes of a football in the NRL went to ground and Brett Mullins scooped it up to run 50 metres for the winning try. No-one was blaming Alfie, of course, I just wish we could have sent him out a winner. As a captain I blame myself a bit for not talking to Bill before the game. When you toss the coin you have a chance to ask the ref if there is anything in particular he is going to be cracking down on. This day I just remember wishing Freddie Fittler good luck and Bill said, 'Let's have a good game.' That was it. I should have asked; maybe he would have told me something which I could have passed on to the boys and we might not have got caned the way we did. I just have to wear it as captain.

We went back into the dressing rooms and went through the usual emotions: disappointment, frustration, and the knowledge that our season had ended one week before we had planned. There was also the knowledge that we had all played our last game with Alfie. It is never the way you want to finish a season, especially at the Broncos, where our expectations and those of our supporters are so high, but sometimes that is just the way it goes.

For me the year wasn't over, though. I had two of the biggest appointments of my life still to come. On 2 November Christine and I were getting married at Hamilton Island. It was a sensational day. We were married in the little chapel there in front of 80 family and close friends. Everything was perfect. The weather was brilliant, Wally was my best man and

Christine's sister Venessa was bridesmaid. Christine looked so beautiful that she took my breath away – literally. My mates will tell you that I'm rarely lost for words, but on this occasion I was. I got up at the reception to speak and I was so emotional I couldn't say a word apart from 'Christine . . .'. Then I just stood there for what seemed like about 15 minutes before sitting down. I had to make it up to her on our honeymoon – 12 days in Mauritius. But before I could concentrate on our wedding plans, there was something else I had to attend to: captaining Australia in a Test match.

WAYNE BENNETT: He's got what Allan Langer had and what Wally Lewis had: blokes want to play with him. You can't get a bigger rap than that. No matter what I say about the bloke or what anyone else says about the bloke, the biggest rap any footballer can get is that people want to play with them.

12 October 2002

We were in a hotel room in Wellington, New Zealand, and Arthur Beetson and Bob McCarthy were handing me a jersey. Not just any jersey, the Australian Test captain's jersey.

We do that before every Test: a former player will hand out the jumpers to the debutantes and, as it was my first Test as captain, I was included. I don't know if it was planned that way or just coincidence, but for me to get my first captain's jersey from Arthur Beetson and Bob McCarthy was a very special experience. When people talk about the greatest players to have played second row – the position I play –

Arthur and Bob are top of the list. I went up and shook their hands and just looked at the jumper. I wonder what odds you would have got five years earlier that I would ever captain Australia in a Test. I know I was never convinced it would happen, even though I had been vice-captain for a few years. When Joey Johns had pulled out with a back injury before that one-off Test against New Zealand I was probably the logical replacement, but logic has never played a big part in my career. As soon as the job came up the media started pushing for Darren Lockyer or Trent Barrett, so I wasn't getting my hopes up. And when I did get the call I wasn't sure whether I'd be able to play. I had been carrying a groin injury for about six weeks and just getting through. Then, late in the game against the Roosters, it really went. I knew I needed an operation but I thought I might be able to get through the Test. It didn't look good. I was having physiotherapy every day but it didn't seem to be doing much good. In a situation like that you are torn. How many chances does a bloke like me get to captain his country? At the same time you don't want to let the team down by going off early and leaving them a man short. I was so doubtful I told Christine and my family not to bother coming over because I didn't think I'd be playing.

The Test was on a Saturday night, and on the Thursday night I went to Chris Anderson and told him I couldn't play. 'Mate,' I said. 'It's hopeless. I can't run, I'm pulling out.' Chris was so supportive. He said, 'Gordie, this is a great honour, don't pass it up easily. We've got a good bench, we can cover you if we have to. Just give it until the last minute and see how you feel.' Those last couple of days did the trick. The physio started to work and I knew that even though I wouldn't be 100 per cent, I would be able to take the ball up and tackle, so I told Chris I'd give it my best shot.

The Test captain's jersey is different from all the others. It has some words embroidered on the inside of the collar. No-one else gets to see them, but just to know they are there is a great feeling. After Beetso and Bob had handed me the jumper I looked out at the newcomers – Craig Wing, Craig Fitzgibbon and Hazem El Masri – and the rest of the boys and said a few words. I've never been one to talk much before a game, it's just not my go, but that night I said what I felt when I'd got that jersey in my hands.

'Fellas, every Test jersey is very special, but they won't mean as much to us if we lose. Let's not just take them home and stick them in the wardrobe. I know I'm very honoured to have this jersey and I want to make it a winning jersey. I want it to be a jersey to be proud of.'

Before the game New Zealand captain Stacey Jones and I went out to toss the coin. I knew the Kiwis were going to be very tough to beat. Most of them had just played in the Grand Final for the Warriors. They were match fit and had something to prove after losing to the Roosters. Some of our blokes hadn't played for weeks. We were coming down after a long season and a lot of us were carrying injuries, so I knew we were up against it. Bill Harrigan was refereeing, and after the way he had treated us in the game against the Roosters I wasn't taking any chances. After the toss I said to him, 'Anything different tonight, Bill?' 'No,' he said. 'Same as last time.' I couldn't help myself. 'Oh,' I said, 'So it'll be 8–1 against us then.' Bill didn't see the funny side but Stacey started laughing. 'Don't worry,' he said to me, 'he stitched us up in the Grand Final too.'

When I walked out onto the field I wasn't thinking about what I was going to do. I never do. I do my preparation as well as I can during the week and what happens on the field happens. This time round I knew I wasn't 100 per cent fit, so in that respect I was a bit disappointed. When you go out for a game like that, captaining your country in a Test for the first time, you'd love to be at your absolute best, but it wasn't to be. All I could think was, 'I'm captaining Australia.'

I know when something like this happens you are supposed to say, 'It was a dream come true', but for me it wasn't. To be honest, I had never dreamed of captaining Australia in a Test because it was so far from my expectations. When I was a kid I dreamed of playing rugby league all right, but my dreams were of playing first grade for Centrals in Townsville. I looked up to the top players in Townsville so much. I thought they were the best players in the game, and if I could just do what they were doing, maybe even play Foley Shield for Townsville in front of a big crowd of 7000 or 8000 people like my Dad had, that would do me.

But you know what they say, the more you get the more you want, and this great game has given me so much. The first time I played first grade for the St George Dragons, even though it was only for a few minutes, I wanted more. When I played in a losing Grand Final I knew I wanted to play in a winning one. Every kid in Queensland wants to play State of Origin. You think if you can get there, just once, you'll die happy. But once isn't enough. You want to know what it is like to win a game, then win a series. You want to have the feeling of being around the best players in the world as much as you can.

Then, if you are really lucky you get to play for Australia

and maybe even, as I did that night in New Zealand, get to captain your country.

The Kiwis came out just as we knew they would, totally pumped up. The first time Shane Webcke took the ball up they hammered him, and from then on we got belted. At one stage we were down 18–6 but we didn't panic. I knew if we could just hold the ball we'd be okay, and that's what happened. After being behind 24–16 at half-time we won 32–24.

As I walked off I felt fantastic. We'd done what we set out to do – win a tough Test match against a good side. There was relief that we'd finished on top and kept Australia's great record intact, and a feeling of satisfaction that we'd fought hard and won.

I went into the dressing room, pulled my phone out of my bag and went outside into the tunnel to ring Christine. We did the media interviews, had some cheers and laughs and backslapping in the dressing room and soaked up the atmosphere of some of the best feelings you can have in sport.

When it had all calmed down I sat on the bench and brushed the dirt off the white 'Raging Poddy Calf' boots so I could get them back into the country, and folded my jersey to put it in my bag.

I looked down at the words stitched into the collar.

'Gorden Tallis. Test captain.'

Yeah. It was a jersey to be proud of.

NEWK
John Newcombe

John Newcombe has always been more than a tennis player – he is an Australian icon. As a player, he was the world number one, a multiple Wimbledon, US and Australian Open champion, a man who would push himself to the limit and beyond to win. Yet he never (or almost never) lost his sense of humour or fun. When Newk was on court you could tell he loved playing the game, and that made watching him all the more enjoyable.

He's friends with US presidents and media tycoons (George Bush once famously described him as a 'black-belt beer drinker'; his son George W. had had one too many with Newk on the night he was arrested for drink driving, Rupert Murdoch bought Ansett and Channel 10 between sets of tennis with him), yet he's also at home in the pub having a beer or three with his mates. He's a larrikin, but he's also a hugely successful businessman in his own right. He's always enjoyed a party, but cares passionately about his family. In a sport where individualism, not to say outright self-centredness, is the norm, he believes that playing in, or captaining a team in the Davis Cup, is the greatest thing a tennis player can do.

Above all he is a brilliant raconteur, and his memoirs are simply unputdownable, filled with gripping tennis drama, extraordinary stories from both on and off the court, deep insights into life, and above all a humour and warmth that Newk's millions of fans will instantly recognise.

REX
My Life

REX is the autobiography of one of Australia}s best-loved and most colourful personalities – Rex Hunt.

His book is Rex to the core – funny, earthy, refreshingly direct and, above all, deeply inspirational. REX tells the story of a kid who struggled at school, but who found the drive and motivation to carve out a hugely successful career as an Aussie Rules footballer and then as a major media figure. Along the way Rex talks about his years in the police force, his National Service, the ups and downs of his business and professional life, the dramatic legal case against his former manager, his loving family, and of course lots and lots of football and fishing. REX is packed with anecdotes and insights into the worlds of AFL, radio and television and the characters Rex has come across in his extraordinary life.

Whether you know Rex as Australia's most distinctive football caller, as the king of fishing shows or just as one of the best-known faces in the country, you'll love this open, frank, endearing and inspiring story.